AFRIKAKORPS: Rommel's Tropical Army in Original Color

Afrikakorps

ROMMEL'S TROPICAL ARMY IN ORIGINAL COLOR

Bernd Peitz
with Gary Wilkins

Schiffer Military History
Atglen, PA

Dedication
To the Soldiers of all Armies who fought in Africa.

Book design by Robert Biondi

Library of Congress Control Number: 2004109580.

ISBN: 978-0-7643-2140-5
Printed in China

Schiffer Books are available at special discounts for bulk purchases for sales promotions or premiums. Special editions, including personalized covers, corporate imprints, and excerpts can be created in large quantities for special needs. For more information contact the publisher:

Published by Schiffer Publishing Ltd.
4880 Lower Valley Road
Atglen, PA 19310
Phone: (610) 593-1777; Fax: (610) 593-2002
E-mail: Info@schifferbooks.com

For the largest selection of fine reference books on this and related subjects, please visit our web site at **www.schifferbooks.com**
We are always looking for people to write books on new and related subjects. If you have an idea for a book please contact us at the above address.

This book may be purchased from the publisher.
Include $5.00 for shipping.
Please try your bookstore first.
You may write for a free catalog.

In Europe, Schiffer books are distributed by
Bushwood Books
6 Marksbury Ave.
Kew Gardens
Surrey TW9 4JF England
Phone: 44 (0) 20 8392 8585; Fax: 44 (0) 20 8392 9876
E-mail: info@bushwoodbooks.co.uk
Website: www.bushwoodbooks.co.uk

Contents

Foreword

I have known the author of this book, Bernd Peitz, for many years. As the son of a comrade from the former German *Afrikakorps*, he regularly takes part in our association meetings together with his father. He has assumed the duties of the Custodian of Traditions within the *Afrika* Fellowship of Paderborn. With commendable effort he has gathered together items from our old "desert army": Photos, documents, books, uniforms and pieces of equipment. And so arose, with the support of many old comrades, a noteworthy documentary about our combat action in North Africa. This may sound like a simple job, but in fact it is extremely laborious, since the majority of our *Afrikakorps*, after exemplary service and varying successes – had to capitulate on 12-13 May 1943 in Tunisia before the absolute personnel and materiel superiority of the Allies. For most of us, that meant up to five years of captivity as Prisoners of War.

Cleaned out by Allied souvenir hunters and the long imprisonment, the majority of us were left with hardly any keepsake as a remembrance. Since then more than sixty years have passed, and only a few of those who experienced the battles of those days remain. And in this sense it is all the more gratifying that there are also a few younger people who hold in honour the memory of our internationally well-respected commander, the "Desert Fox" Erwin Rommel and his irreproachably courageous *Afrikakorps*.

Though it subsequently turned out that we were misused in the power politics of a dictator with no conscience, Field Marshal Rommel and us as his soldiers, despite all the harshness of war, always acted honourably toward our opponents.

This mutual respect, and soldierly comradeship then led not long after the war's end, and with the assistance of our former opponents, to the founding of our group "The German Afrikakorps Association." Over the course of the years, enemies of old have become friends.

When Bernd Peitz told me about his book project at one of the latest Association meetings, I was at first very reserved. What new information could he bring forth about the African campaign that had not already been written by someone else – and seeing as how he hadn't even experienced it? But his concept of publishing a photo book based almost entirely on color photographs from that time – as a sort of quasi view into the private photo albums of veterans – really made me sit up and take notice. When he then showed me the photos that had been provided to him by combat Veterans and their families, I felt closer to the events of those days than I have rarely ever felt since. In contrast to black and white pictures, this color material shows vitality, a sense of life that the majority of non-color pictures of the time are unable to impart. Together with the descriptive captions, this book will surely be an enrichment for the Africa Veterans. In addition, this photo documentary also offers the historically interested observer, the uniform collector and model vehicle builder a wealth of information.

Hans-Günther Stark
Former Vice Chairperson of the "Association* of the German *Afrika-Korps*"
Captain (Ret.) – with a Reconnaissance Battalion in Africa

**Officially Registered Association*

Vorwort

Bernd Peitz, der Autor dieses Buches, ist mir seit vielen Jahren bekannt. Als Sohn eines Kameraden vom ehemaligen Deutschen Afrikakorps nimmt er regelmäßig zusammen mit seinem Vater an unseren Verbandstreffen teil. Innerhalb der Afrika-Kameradschaft Paderborn hat er die Aufgabe des Traditionspflegers übernommen. Mit anerkennenswertem Einsatz trägt er Exponate unserer alten Wüstenarmee zusammen: Fotos, Dokumente, Bücher, Uniform- und Ausrüstungsteile. So entstand mit Unterstützung vieler alter Kameraden eine beachtenswerte Dokumentation über unseren Kriegseinsatz in Nordafrika. Dies hört sich zwar einfach an, ist aber in der Tat äußerst mühselig, da der größte Teil unseres Afrikakorps nach beispielhaftem Einsatz und wechselnden Erfolgen, doch vor der absoluten personellen und materiellen Überlegenheit der Alliierten am 12./13.Mai 1943 in Tunesien kapitulieren musste. Das bedeutete für die meisten von uns eine bis zu 5-Jährige Kriegsgefangenschaft. Ausgeplündert durch alliierte Souvenirjäger und die lange Gefangenschaft blieb den meisten Veteranen kaum ein Erinnerungsstück. Inzwischen sind mehr als 60 Jahre vergangen und es leben nur noch wenige von denen die Kampfhandlungen damals miterlebt haben. Umso erfreulicher ist es, dass es auch noch einige Jüngere gibt, die die Erinnerung an unseren international hochgeach-teten Oberbefehlshaber, den "Wüstenfuchs" General-Feldmarschall Erwin Rommel und sein untadelig tapferes Afrikakorps in Ehren halten.

Wenn sich im Nachhinein auch herausgestellt hat, dass wir von einem gewissenlosen Diktator für dessen Machtpolitik missbraucht wurden, so haben Feldmarschall Rommel und wir als seine Soldaten uns trotz aller Härte des Krieges stets ritterlich gegenüber unseren damaligen Kriegsgegnern verhalten. Diese dann auch gegenseitige Achtung und die gute Kameradschaft innerhalb der Truppe führte dann schon wenige Jahre nach Kriegsende unter Mithilfe unserer einstmaligen Gegner zur Gründung unseres Verbandes " Deutsches Afrika-Korps e.V.". Aus den Gegnern von einst wurden im Laufe der Jahre Freunde.

Als mir Bernd Peitz bei einem unserer letzten Verbandstreffen von seinem Buch-Projekt erzählte, war ich erst sehr zurückhaltend. Was will der noch für neue Informationen über den Afrika-Feldzug bringen, was nicht schon andere geschrieben haben und zumal er ihn nicht selbst miterlebt hat? – Aber sein Konzept, einen Bildband mit überwiegend Farbfotos aus der Zeit zu veröffentlichen – quasi als Blick in die privaten Fotoalben von Kriegsveteranen – ließ mich aufhorchen. Als er mir dann noch seine, ihm von Veteranen und deren Familien zur Verfügung gestellten Fotos zeigte, fühlte ich mich dem damaligen Geschehen so nah wie selten zuvor. Im Gegensatz zu schwarz/weiß Fotografien zeigt dieses Farb-Bildmaterial eine Lebendigkeit, die die meisten Fotos aus der Zeit nicht vermitteln können. Zusammen mit den Bilderläuterungen wird dieses Buch sicher eine Bereicherung für Veteranen sein. Desweiteren bietet dieser Farbbildband dem historisch interessierten Betrachter, dem Uniformen-Sammler und dem Fahrzeug-Modellbauer eine Fülle an Informationen.

Hans-Günther Stark
Ehem. 2. Vorsitzender des Verbandes "Deutsches Afrika-Korps e.V."
Hauptmann a.D. – in Afrika bei einer Aufklärungsabteilung

Dedication & Acknowledgments

Dedication

I dedicate this book to my father and his comrades from the former German *Afrikakorps*, their Italian allies, and their military opponents of those times: British, Australians, New Zealanders, Canadians, Indians, South Africans, French and Americans. In a part of the Earth in which they were all foreign, the men of these nations fought with the same patriotism in the deserts of Africa, for the interests of their countries. 100,000 people from the countries taking part in this theater of war lost their lives. May their deaths and suffering be a warning for us, so that we make efforts for a just peace and friendship among all peoples.

Acknowledgments

All of the photos printed in this book have their origin in the private property of the former soldiers of the German *Afrikakorps*. They were very kindly turned over to me by their family members and comrades for my private *Afrikakorps* Tradition-Collection. The majority of the photos come from Eberhard Dohm (deceased), of the *Afrika*-Fellowship Bielefeld, who was a photographer with a propaganda company in Africa, Sicily and Italy. Additional photos come from Richard Wagener (deceased), of the *Afrika*-Fellowship Dortmund, who was in Africa with *Panzer* Regiment 5.

My very special thanks are therefore due to the Dohm family, the Comradeship Bielefeld, Mrs. Erika Prinz, and comrade Erwin Schuth.

Thanks also to my father and to many of his comrades, who commented on photos and described their experiences to me in countless conversations.

I would additionally like to thank: My friend and collecting colleague of many years, Dal McGuirk of New Zealand, author of two books on the German *Afrikakorps: Rommel's Army in Africa*, and *Afrikakorps Self-Portrait*, who imparted a great deal of knowledge to me on the uniforms and equipment of the *Afrikakorps*.

My dear friend Patricia Spayd (USA), author of the biography *Generalleutnant Fritz Bayerlein: From Afrikakorps to Panzer Lehr*, who put me in contact with Schiffer Publishing, Ltd., and who was my "courier" between the USA and Germany.

My translator, Gary Wilkins (USA), author of *The Collector's Guide to Cloth Third Reich Military Headgear* for his outstanding work.

The chief editor (military history) of Schiffer Publishing, Ltd., Bob Biondi, for his courage and patience in attempting such a project with a "literary layman."

Friends, colleagues, and – not to be forgotten – my wife and children, for their assistance of all sorts, and support.

The sense and purpose of this book is not to be an "Umpteenth Chronology" of the African campaign. This has been written about very often, and those with interest can find extensive literature available on the subject. I would much prefer it to be understood as a view, of sorts into the private photo albums of war veterans, and as such to impart to the reader the same sense of wonder that befell me when I saw the first color pictures of the African campaign.

In general, we know only black and white photos from this time period – which push the war into a distant past. The pictures before you, however, were taken with a color slide technique rarely used at that time, and impart to us a substantially more lively image of those days. They offer Veterans a look into the years of their youth; give those with an interest in history – collectors, re-enactors and model builders – genuine moments that were frozen in time. The two photographers Eberhard Dohm and Richard Wagener took these photos in those days as a personal remembrance, and the photos show what the two of them saw and experienced. These are *not* shots posed in a mission for the *Reichs* Propaganda Ministry.

The viewer of these pictures can understand of course, that there is not a picture present for every person or object that may be of interest – I can only pass on the pictures that were taken, and which survived intact. Some reduction in quality must also be accepted in part, as the technical level of the times was not that far along and the photos also have undergone an aging process. I have left out a considerable amount of material on folklore like Bedouins, camels, palm trees, and ancient ruins, since this book is not intended to be a Tourist Guide to North Africa.

A number of Eberhard Dohm's black and white photos have also been included, since with the difficult supply situation of the *Afrikakorps* it is understandable that color film was not always available.

As a supplement to the historical chronology, I have brought together in the final section of the book a number of color photos of the subsequent fighting on Sicily. The photos were identified in "keyword" fashion. From these scanty statements I then developed the captions based on a consideration of specific equipment characteristics. If I have run afoul of misinterpretation, or if you are able to identify other individuals in the pictures, then I would be very pleased if you would contact me through Schiffer Publishing, Ltd., 4880 Lower Valley Road, Atglen, PA 19310, USA.

Bernd Peitz
Custodian of Traditions for the Afrika-Fellowship,
Paderborn in the Association of the German *Afrika-Korps* e.V.*

**Officially Registered Association – Transl.*

Widmung

Dieses Buch widme ich meinem Vater und seinen Kameraden vom ehemaligen Deutschen Afrikakorps, ihren italienischen Verbündeten und den damaligen Kriegsgegnern: Briten, Australier, Neuseeländer, Canadier, Inder, Süd-Afrikaner, Franzosen und Amerikaner.

Männer all dieser Nationen kämpften in der Wüste Nordafrikas mit dem gleichen Patriotismus für die Interessen ihrer Nationen – in diesem Teil der Erde in dem sie alle Fremde waren.

Auf diesem Kriegsschauplatz liessen etwa 100.000 Menschen aller beteiligten Staaten ihr Leben. Möge uns ihr Leiden und Tod eine Mahnung sein, damit wir uns um einen gerechten Frieden und Freundschaft unter allen Völkern bemühen.

Dank: Alle in diesem Buch abgebildeten Fotos stammen aus dem Privatbesitz von ehemaligen Soldaten des deutschen Afrikakorps. Sie wurden mir freundlicherweise von ihren Familien und Kameraden für meine private Afrikakorps Traditions-Sammlung überlassen.

Die meisten dieser Fotos stammen von Eberhard Dohm†, Afrika-Kamerad-schaft Bielefeld, der in Afrika, Sizilien und Italien Fotograph bei einer Propagandakompanie war.

Weitere Fotos stammen von Richard Wagener†, Afrika-Kameradschaft Dortmund, der in Afrika beim Panzer Regiment 5 war.

Mein ganz besonderer Dank gilt deshalb der Familie Dohm, der Afrika Kameradschaft Bielefeld, Frau Erika Prinz und Kamerad Erwin Schuth.

Dank aber auch meinem Vater und vielen seiner Kameraden, die mir in zahllosen Gesprächen ihre Erlebnisse in Nord-Afrika schilderten und Fotos erläuterten.

Desweiteren danke ich:

Meinem langjährigen Freund und Sammelkollegen Dal Mc Guirk aus Neu-Seeland (Autor von zwei Büchern über das Deutsche Afrikakorps: Rommels Army in Africa und Afrikakorps Selfportrait), der mir sehr viel Wissen über Uniformen und Ausrüstung des Afrikakorps vermittelt hat.

Meiner lieben Freundin Patricia Spayd, USA, (Autorin der Biografie von General Bayerlein: From Afrikakorps to Panzer Lehr) die mich mit dem Schiffer Verlag in Kontakt brachte und mein "Kurier" zwischen den USA und Deutschland war.

Meinem Übersetzer Gary Wilkins, USA, (Autor von: The Collectors Guide to Cloth Third Reich Military Headgear) für seine hervorragende Arbeit.

Dem Chefredakteur Herrn Bob Biondi vom Schiffer Verlag für seinen Mut und Nachsicht ein solches Projekt mit einem schriftstellerischen Laien zu wagen.

Freunde, Kollegen und nicht zu vergessen meine Frau und meine Kinder für ihre vielfältige Hilfe und Unterstützung.

Sinn und Zweck dieses Buches soll nicht die x-ste Chronologie des Afrika-Feldzuges sein.

Darüber wurde schon sehr oft geschrieben und der Interessierte findet dazu umfangreiche Literatur. Vielmehr möchte ich es quasi als Blick in die privaten Fotoalben von Kriegs-veteranen verstanden wissen und Ihnen die gleiche Begeisterung vermitteln die mich befiel, als ich die ersten dieser Farbfotos vom Afrika-Feldzug sah. Im Allgemeinen kennen wir aus dieser Zeit nur schwarz/weiss Fotos, die diesen Krieg in eine ferne Vergangenheit rücken. Diese Fotos sind jedoch in der damals noch selten angewandten Farb-Dia Technik aufgenommen worden und vermitteln uns ein wesentlich lebendigeres Bild aus längst vergangenen Zeiten.

Den Veteranen ein Blick in ihre Jugendjahre, den historisch Interessierten, Sammlern, Re-enactorn und Modellbauern unverfälschte Momentaufnahmen aus der Vergangenheit.

Die beiden Fotografen Eberhard Dohm und Richard Wagener haben diese Fotos damals als persönliche Andenken aufgenommen und zeigen das von ihnen Erlebte und Gesehene.

Es sind also keine gestellten Aufnahmen im Auftrag des Reichs-Propaganda-ministeriums. Der Betrachter dieser Bilder möge allerdings verstehen, das nicht zu jeder ihn interessierenden Person oder Objekt ein Foto vorhanden ist, ich kann nur das weitergeben, was aufgenommen wurde und erhalten blieb. Teilweise müssen auch Abstriche in der Qualität hingenommen werden, denn die Technik war damals noch nicht soweit und das Fotomaterial unterlag zudem Alterungsprozessen. Ich habe etliches an Folklore wie Beduinen, Kamele, Palmen und antike Ruinen weggelassen, denn dieses Buch soll ja kein Touristenführer für Nord-Afrika sein.

Es wurden auch etliche schwarz/weiss Fotos von Eberhard Dohm mitverwandt denn bei der schwierigen Nachschublage beim Afrikakorps ist es verständlich, das nicht immer Farbfilme zur Verfügung standen. Im letzen Teil des Buches habe ich als Ergänzung der geschichtlichen Chronologie noch etliche Farbfotos von den anschliessenden Kämpfen auf der Insel Sizilien mit eingebracht.

Die Fotos waren zum Teil stichpunktartig beschrieben. Aus diesen knappen Angaben habe ich dann die Textbeschreibungen unter Berücksichtigung ausrüstungsspezifischer Besonderheiten entwickelt. Sollte ich hierbei Fehldeutungen erlegen sein, oder sie können noch abgebildete Personen identifizieren, würde ich mich freuen, wenn sie über den Schiffer-Verlag mit mir Kontakt aufnehmen würden.

Bernd Peitz
Traditionspfleger der Afrika-Kameradschaft Paderborn
im "Verband Deutsches Afrika-Korps" e.V.

Translator's Note

Translating is never an exact science. As with the very nature of language itself, translating is a subjective endeavour. The translator's job is to interpret the intentions and mood of the author through the translation with as little "translation loss" as possible, and carry these across to the reader. Many readers may believe that translations are done on a word for word, literal basis, when in fact, this is almost never the case: such a method usually comes across as extremely stilted in the target language (i.e. English). In many languages – German among them – a specific phrase, or expression often cannot be translated directly into English using the same form as the original. The translator's job, then, is to make an analytical – but at the same time subjective – decision, and choose an English phrase that most closely (and accurately) imparts the nuances that the book's author intended with the native (i.e. the "Source") text, and sometimes only a completely different English expression or grammatical structure will serve to convey the majority of the original German meaning, or nuance. For those English-speaking readers who wish to try out their own German skills, dual language books like this one provide a unique opportunity for study – and a wealth of military terms with which to enhance your vocabulary skills.

Another important task of the translator is to make certain decisions regarding whether a word should be translated at all – or left in the original language. For example, in the captions I have chosen *not* to translate *Afrikakorps/Afrika-Korps*, since the German word is clearly understandable in English. Panzer (tank), also remains likewise untranslated *in most cases*, as it is probably the single most familiar German military word to any English speakers possessing even a little knowledge of the German Army – and it is a word with an impact that I feel is best portrayed in the original language. So to, with other words such as *Infanterie* (infantry) and *Artillerie* (artillery), since these terms – even with German spellings – are all recognizable in English.

In some cases I did not translate the German words *Luftwaffe* (Air Force), or *Flak* (Anti-aircraft Gun) in the text if they were not a critical part of the information – because these words again are already quite familiar to many English Speakers. *Flak* in fact, is a German military acronym for *Fliegerabwehr Kanone* – antiaircraft cannon/gun – that found its way into the English language: use of the acronym originated during World War II among the Allied aircrews who daily challenged the intense German anti-aircraft (i.e. *Flak*) fire in the skies over Europe. The now slightly antiquated colloquial expression "catch Flak" slipped for many years into everyday speech as an idiom, for example: *I caught flak from the boss for that* – with the German military origin quickly being forgotten (most people were never aware of it's origin.* This idiom has mostly been retired from English usage today, bumped out of favour by newer expressions. The word *Flak* is slowly fading away.

The photo captions in this book identify a considerable amount of information on various forms of German military uniform and equipment, which not all readers may be familiar with. A brief glossary is provided at the back of the book for the convenience of anyone wishing to refresh his or her memory of the terminology, or interested in learning a little more about an item.

I would like to thank Bill Shea, owner of The Ruptured Duck website (www.therupturedduck.com), for providing some very useful technical assistance regarding clarification of the uniform entries in the glossary. Thanks also once again, to Marlen and Dieter Hundrieser in Germany: true friends indeed!

My primary objective with this translation was to convey to the reader the same sense of historical fascination and closeness to the events that Bernd portrays in the German original, and I hope in this to have succeeded.

Gary Wilkins
Translator/Editor
Boston, July 2004

** Another example: Have you ever wondered where the word „skosh" (meaning, 'a little') comes from in the expression „just a skosh"? This word was almost certainly a Veteran bring-back by members of the U.S. occupation forces (civilian and military) stationed in Japan after the war. Many of these personnel learned a few words and phrases in the local lingo in order to "get by" after official work hours, when out on the town. One of the more frequently used Japanese words was „skoshi" – meaning 'small', or 'little'. The word was easy to pronounce and had a bit of a ring to it; many of the soldiers, airmen and occupation staff picked it up and used it in their daily English conversation as well – then brought it back home with them upon their return, at which time the word made its way into general usage. This Japanese word, albeit slightly shortened to "skosh" from the original, fares better than the German word „flak" since it is still in use – though once again with its foreign origin completely forgotten.*

The African Campaign: A Short Overview

On 13 September 1940, an Italian Army group started an offensive from their North African colony of Libya against the weak British border security in their colony of Egypt. After taking about 100km of terrain, the offensive ground to a halt on 18 September in the area of Sidi Barrani. Heavily outnumbered, but with technically much better equipped forces, the British started a counter offensive at the beginning of December 1940, which turned into a fiasco for the Italians. After only a week the British had driven them back out of Egypt and now chased the fleeing Italians into Libyan territory. On 22 January, after taking approximately 150 kilometers of terrain, they captured the fortress and harbour of Tobruk. After overrunning a total of approximately 800km of terrain along the Libyan coastline, and the conquest of additional cities like Derna and Benghazi, the British offensive stalled due to supply problems in the area around El Agheila on 8 February 1941. In trade for a few losses, they had taken around 130,000 Italian prisoners up to that time, and bagged large quantities of military equipment. In desperation the Italian dictator Mussolini turned to his close [Axis] alliance partner, the German dictator Adolf Hitler, and requested military assistance from him. As an immediate stopgap, several German *Luftwaffe* units were transferred to Sicily in order to disrupt the British advance in Libya and to attack the British convoy escorts in the Mediterranean. From 1 February 1941, the first German soldiers arrived in Libya to support their hard-pressed Italian ally in the battle against the British on land.

In the belief that they were serving their people here as well, they fought with exemplary courage under the command of the legendary *General* Erwin Rommel. They were usually inferior to the Allies in terms of equipment and personnel, since for Hitler this was only a sideshow; the Eastern Front swallowed up his divisions and war material. Of the little that was left to the North African Theater the British sent a substantial portion to the bottom of the Mediterranean. Nothing remained to Rommel but to employ as much captured equipment as possible, and to make use of ruses to fool the enemy about his actual strength.

From the Italian side only a few combat capable units – and those with outdated equipment – stood available. After varying success they had nonetheless managed to push the British and their allies back to Egypt and to within 100km of Alexandria and the Nile Delta. Here the British had set up a final, strong defensive line at the small place of El Alamein, where the German *Afrikakorps* was brought to a halt. A breakthrough of this line was no longer possible with their degraded units; the German side had hardly any operational *Panzers* remaining and this was the primary weapon for such an offensive. A detour to the south around this blockade line was not possible due to the adjacent Katarra Depression with its quicksand fields and salt marshes.

While urgently needed re-supply was awaited on the German side, which arrived only with exceptional sparcity, the British under their new General Bernard Montgomery concentrated their efforts on just this point and succeeded in bringing in large quantities of materiel and fresh troops.

In the night of 23-24 October 1942 the British opened their counter offensive against the German positions with a five-hour barrage from 1000 pieces of artillery, to which little response could be made from the German side as there was hardly any ammunition on hand. In a tough, ten-day long struggle with the desperately defending Germans and Italians, the vastly superior British, in the meantime, had managed to breakthrough the Axis lines, taking 30,000 prisoners. Against Hitler's order to stand fast, Rommel ordered a withdrawal back to defensive positions in order to save the *Afrikakorps* from imminent destruction.

The situation intensified dramatically when only a few days later, on 7 and 8 November 1942, American troops landed in Morocco and Algeria. Rommel, and finally the General

Staff and Hitler as well, recognized the danger of the complete loss of North Africa. While Rommel commanded the orderly withdrawal to Tunisia in order to build a bridgehead there, a large number of reserves were carried across to Tunisia in great haste by the German leadership, in order to get there ahead of the Americans. By the end of January 1943, German and Italian troops had withdrawn completely into Tunisia.

While the British probed carefully along the Tunisian-Libyan border, the American advance in the Tunisian-Algerian border zone was checked. Rommel wanted to lead his troops from there back to Italy, but this was strictly refused by the German high command. On the 9th of March *Generalfeldmarschall* Rommel, who was totally exhausted physically, was relieved by *Generaloberst*[*] von Arnim.

Bitter fighting flared again. On the German side, everything possible was done to hold the Tunisian bridgehead, but this was fated to fail from the beginning due to the immense personnel and material re-supply of the Allies. Step by step, the bridgehead was squeezed ever tighter. On the 12th and 13th of May 1943, the remainder of the German/Italian *Afrikakorps* finally capitulated. Falling into Allied hands as POWs were 130,000 German and 120,000 Italian soldiers. The last of the Africa fighters were only released after five years of captivity, in May of 1948.

[*] *U.S. Rank: General (4 Stars) – Transl.*

Der Afrika-Feldzug: Geschichtlicher Überblick

Am 13 September 1940 startete eine italienische Heeresgruppe von ihrer nordafrikanischen Kolonie Libyen aus eine Offensive gegen die schwachen britischen Grenzsicherungen in deren Kolonie Ägypten. Nach einem Geländegewinn von etwa 100 km blieb die Offensive am 18. September im Raum Sidi Barrani stecken. Anfang Dezember 1940 traten die Briten mit zahlenmäßig zwar weit unterlegenen aber technisch besser ausgerüsteten Kräften eine Gegenoffensive an, die für die Italiener zu einem Fiasko wurde. Schon nach einer Woche hatten die Briten die Italiener wieder aus Ägypten vertrieben und setzten nun den flüchtenden Italienern auf libyschem Gebiet nach. Am 22. Januar 1941 eroberten sie nach einem Geländegewinn von etwa 150 km die Festung und den Hafen von Tobruk. Nach insgesamt etwa 800 km Geländegewinn entlang der lybischen Küstenlinie, unter Eroberung weiterer Städte wie Derna und Bengasi, blieb die britische Offensive wegen Nachschubproblemen am

8. Februar 1941 im Raum El Agheila stecken. Bis dahin hatten sie bei geringen eigenen Verlusten etwa 130.000 Italiener gefangen genommen und große Mengen Kriegsgerät erbeutet. In seiner Not wandte sich der italienische Diktator Benito Mussolini an seinen Bündnispartner, dem deutschen Diktator Adolf Hitler, und bat ihn um Waffenhilfe. Als Sofortmaßnahme wurden einige Deutsche Luftwaffenverbände nach Sizilien verlegt, um den britischen Vormarsch in Libyen zu stören und um britische Geleitzüge im Mittelmeer anzugreifen. Ab Februar 1941 kamen die ersten deutschen Soldaten nach Libyen um ihre arg bedrängten italienischen Bündnispartner auch zu Lande im Kampf gegen die Briten zu unterstützen.

Im Glauben auch hier ihrem Volk zu dienen, kämpften sie mit beispielhafter Tapferkeit unter dem Kommando des legendären Generals Erwin Rommel. Personal- und materialmäßig waren sie den Alliierten meist unterlegen, denn für Hitler war dies nur ein Nebenkriegsschauplatz – die Ostfront verschlang seine Divisionen und Kriegsgerät. Von dem wenigen was für den nordafrikanischen Kriegsschauplatz übrig blieb, versenkten die Briten noch einen nicht unerheblichen Teil auf den Grund des Mittelmeeres. So blieb Rommel nichts anderes übrig, als auch Beutematerial in großem Umfang einzusetzen und sich Kriegslisten zu bedienen um den Gegner über seine tatsächliche Stärke zu täuschen.

Von italienischer Seite standen ihm nur wenige kampfkräftige, zudem noch mit veraltetem Gerät ausgestattete Einheiten, zur Verfügung. Nach wechselnden Erfolgen hatten sie es trotzdem geschafft die Briten und ihre Verbündeten weit nach Ägypten bis etwa 100 km vor Alexandria und dem Nildelta zurückzudrängen. Hier hatten die Briten bei der kleinen Ortschaft El Alamein eine letzte starke Verteidigungsstellung errichtet, an der das deutsche Afrikakorps zum Halten gebracht wurde. Ein Durchbrechen dieser Linie war mit den abgekämpften Einheiten nicht mehr möglich, zumal auf deutscher Seite kaum noch einsatzbereite Panzer – der Hauptwaffe für eine derartige Offensive – zur Verfügung standen. Ein Umgehen dieser Sperrlinie im Süden war unmöglich, da sich hier die für Fahrzeuge unpassierbare Katarra-Senke mit ihren Treibsandfeldern und Salzsümpfen anschließt.

Während auf deutscher Seite mal wieder auf den dringend benötigten Nachschub gewartet wurde, der nur äußerst spärlich eintraf, konzentrierten die Briten unter ihrem neuen Oberbefehlshaber General Bernard Montgomery ihre Anstrengungen auf diesen Punkt und schafften große Mengen an Material und frischen Truppen hierher.

In der Nacht vom 23. auf den 24. Oktober 1942 eröffneten die Briten mit einem fünfstündigen Trommelfeuer aus 1000 Artillerie-Geschützen auf die deutschen Stellungen ihre Gegenoffensive, dem von deutscher Seite nichts nennenswertes mehr entgegengesetzt werden konnte, da kaum noch Munition vorhanden war. In einem zehntägigen harten Ringen mit den sich verzweifelt wehrenden deutsch-italienischen Truppen gelang es den inzwischen weit überlegenen Briten die Linien der Achsenmächte zu durchbrechen und etwa 30.000 Soldaten gefangen zu nehmen. Entgegen dem Haltebefehl Hitlers befahl Rommel den Rückzug in Auffangstellungen, um das Afrikakorps vor der drohenden Vernichtung zu bewahren.

Die Situation verschärfte sich dramatisch, als wenige Tage später am 7./8. November 1942 amerikanische Truppen in Marokko und Algerien landeten. Rommel und endlich auch Hitler und der deutsche Generalstab erkannten die Gefahr des kompletten Verlustes von Nord-Afrika.

Während Rommel den geordneten Rückzug Richtung Tunesien befahl um dort einen Brückenkopf zu bilden, wurden von der deutschen Führung in grosser Eile Reserveeinheiten nach Tunesien überführt um den Amerikanern zuvorzukommen. Bis Ende Januar 1943 hatten sich die Deutsch/italienischen Truppen komplett nach Tunesien zurückgezogen.

Während die Briten im tunesisch/libyschen Grenzgebiet vorsichtig nachstießen, war der amerikanische Vorstoss im tunesisch/algerischen Grenzgebiet aufgehalten worden.

Rommel wollte seine Truppen von dort nach Italien zurückführen, was aber von der deutschen Führung strikt abgelehnt wurde. Am 9. März wurde der gesundheitlich total erschöpfte GFM Rommel durch Generaloberst von Arnim abgelöst.

Wieder entbrannten erbitterte Gefechte. Auf deutscher Seite wurde alles versucht um den tunesischen Brückenkopf zu halten, was aber wegen des imensen Personal- und Materialnachschubs der Alliierten von Anfang an zum Scheitern verurteilt war. Zug um Zug wurde der Brückenkopf von den Alliierten eingeengt. Am 12./13. Mai kapitulierten schliesslich die Reste des deutsch/italienischen Afrikakorps. 130.000 deutsche und 120.000 italienische Soldaten gerieten in alliierte Kriegsgefangenschaft, woraus die letzten Afrikakämpfer erst im Mai 1948 nach 5-jähriger Gefangenschaft entlassen wurden.

The Photographs

The harbour of the Libyan capitol, Tripoli in 1941; in the background are the dock facilities.

Der Hafen der libyschen Hauptstadt Tripolis 1941 – im Bildhintergrund die Dockanlagen.

The first German combat units – Reconnaissance Battalion 3, and Anti-tank Battalion 39 – set foot on African soil on 13 February 1941. In the following weeks other units were moved to Tripoli. On the 28th of February, the *Panzer* regiment (*Pz.Rgt.5*) was uploaded on railway flatcars in Berlin, and brought to Italy. In Naples, the regiment was then loaded onto four freighters and with an accompanying escort reached the harbour of Tripoli on 10 March, where it was unloaded immediately. In the left background the photo shows a group of *Panzer* soldiers watching the unloading of the ships. The fact that they are still wearing the black [**Continental Panzer uniform in black wool. – Transl.*] uniform is noteworthy. In the foreground, native dockworkers are busy unloading heavy bombs for aircraft.

Am 13. Februar 1941 betraten die ersten deutschen Kampfeinheiten, die Aufklärungsabteilung 3 und die Panzerjägerabt. 39, in Tripolis afrikanischen Boden. In den folgenden Wochen wurden weitere Verbände nach Tripolis verlegt. Am 28. Februar wurde das Panzer Regiment 5 (Pz Rgt 5) in Wünsdorf bei Berlin auf Eisenbahn-Waggons verladen und nach Italien gebracht. In Neapel wurde das Pz Rgt dann auf 4 Frachtschiffe verladen und erreichte mit Geleitschutz am 10. März den Hafen von Tripolis, wo unverzüglich entladen wurde. Das Foto zeigt im linken Bildhintergrund eine Gruppe Panzersoldaten, die der Entladung der Schiffe zusehen. Auffällig ist, dass sie noch die schwarzen Uniformen tragen. Im Bildvordergrund sind einheimische Hafenarbeiter mit der Entladung schwerer Fliegerbomben beschäftigt.

10 March 1941. Pz.Rgt. 5 in formation in Tripoli. At this time, the Regiment was comprised of seven armored command vehicles [presumably Sd.Kfz.'s*], twenty-five *Panzer* [model] 1 tanks, forty-five *Panzer* II's, fifty-one *Panzer* III's and seventeen *Panzer* IV's. On the left is a medical halftrack with the Red Cross symbol. [**See the Glossary under "Vehicles" for more information on these vehicles.*]

12. März 1941. Das Pz Rgt 5 ist zur Parade in Tripolis angetreten. Das Regiment verfügte zu diesem Zeitpunkt über 7 Panzerbefehlswagen, 25 Panzer I, 45 Panzer II, 51 Panzer III und 17 Panzer IV. Links ein Sanitäts-Schützenpanzer mit dem Rot-Kreuz Symbol.

In the foreground is a *Panzer* III with the short 50mm cannon. The tanks are painted in the standard *Wehrmacht* "gray". The unit recognition symbol, an upside down "Y" with two lines, can be easily seen. At that time, this symbol was the identifying mark for the 3rd *Panzer* Division, to which *Panzer* Regiment 5 belonged before the African campaign. Behind the tanks stands a *Major* (center) and two Lieutenants, who are officially wearing the new tropical uniform here for the first time. They wear the standard (contintental) officer's collar tab and shoulder board rank insignia. They have taken the Hussars skull from the black [*Panzer*] uniform as well. Of particular note is that the *Major* is wearing an enlisted man's tropical breast eagle sewn to his tunic. For headgear, they are wearing the new tropical field cap [*M-41*], which was developed from the mountain cap [*Bergmütze*] used by mountain troops. The officer version of this cap had silver piping around the crown, and the simulated front scallop (*Generals* wore gold piping). In addition to the national emblem (eagle) and the cockade, the caps have a pink inverted "V" soutache chevron (pink was the branch color for *Panzer* personnel).

Im Vordergrund ein Panzer III mit der kurzen 5 cm Kanone. Die Panzer sind noch in dem bei der Wehrnacht sonst üblichen "Panzer-grau" lackiert. Gut zu sehen ist hier das Truppenkennzeichen, ein umgedrehtes Y mit 2 Strichen. Dieses Symbol war zu der Zeit das Kennzeichen der 3. Panzer Division, zu der das Pz Rgt 5 vor dem Afrika-Feldzug gehörte. Hinter dem Panzer stehen ein Major (mitte) und zwei Oberleutnants, die hier erstmalig offiziell die neue Tropen-Uniform tragen. An ihren olivgrünen Feldblusen tragen sie die regulären Offiziers-Rangabzeichen Schulterklappen und Kragenspiegel. Von den Kragenspiegeln der schwarzen Panzer-Uniform haben sie zusätzlich die Totenkopfabzeichen übernommen. Auffällig ist allerdings, dass an der Feldbluse des Majors ein Hoheitsadler in der Tropenausführung für Mannschaftsdienstgrade aufgenäht wurde. Als Kopfbedeckung tragen sie die neuen Tropen-Feldmützen, die aus der Bergmütze der Gebirgsjäger entwickelt wurde. Die Offiziers-Ausführung dieser Mütze hat eine eingenähte silberne Litze um das Mützenoberteil und dem nur angedeuteten vorderen Umschlag (Generäle goldene Litze). Neben dem Hoheitsadler und der Kokarde zeigt die Mützenfront einen rosa Soutache-Winkel (rosa ist die Waffenfarbe der Panzertruppe).

A group of *Panzer* soldiers with an Arab in front of their tank. From left to right is a sergeant, a 2nd Lieutenant, an NCO, the Arab, and another NCO. These soldiers have proven themselves in several battles in Poland and France – they already wear the *Panzer* Assault Badge [*Panzerkampfabzeichen*[*]], which was awarded after three successful tank battles, and several even wear the ribbon for the Iron Cross 2nd Class [*Eisernes Kreuz II. Klasse – commonly referred to as the "EK II"*[*]]. While the Lieutenant wears the officer's version of the field cap described previously and a double-claw belt, the enlisted men are equipped with the newly introduced tropical overseas cap and the Other Ranks webbed belt and buckle. The tank bears the number 521, which represents the 5th Company, 2nd Platoon, Tank No. 1. This is the vehicle of the Lieutenant commanding the 2nd platoon of the 5th company. Behind it is a tank of the 6th company. [*[*]See the Glossary under "Awards."*]

Eine Gruppe Panzersoldaten mit einem Araber vor ihrem Panzer. Von links nach rechts sehen wir: Einen Feldwebel, einen Leutnant, einen Unteroffizier, den Araber und einen weiteren Unteroffizier (Uffz.). Diese Soldaten haben sich schon in mehreren Panzergefechten in Polen oder Frankreich bewährt. Sie tragen bereits das silberne Panzer-Kampfabzeichen, welches nach erfolgreicher Bewährung in 3 Panzergefechten verliehen wurde und einige sogar die Bandspange zum Eisernen Kreuz 2. Klasse. Während der Leutnant die zuvor schon beschriebene Offiziers-Ausführung der Feldmütze und einen Ledergürtel mit 2-Dorn-Schliesse trägt, sind die Mannschaftsdienstgrade mit der ebenfalls neu eingeführten Tropen-"Schiffchenmütze" und dem Mannschaftskoppel mit Webstoffriemen und Kastenschloss ausgestattet. Der Panzer trägt die Nummer 521. Das bedeutet: 5. Kompanie, 2. Zug, Wagen 1 = dies ist der Panzer des Zugführers des 2. Zugs der 5. Kompanie. Dahinter ist ein Panzer II der 6. Kompanie zu sehen.

The same group of tankers, beside their vehicle. Of particular note is that all are wearing breeches (a type of riding pants) and the tropical lace-up boots.

Die selbe Gruppe Panzersoldaten neben ihrem Panzer. Auffällig ist, dass alle Breeches-Hosen (eine Art Reithose) tragen und dazu die hohen Tropen-Schnürstiefel.

A tanker in front of his *Panzer* III.

Ein Panzersoldat vor seinem Panzer III.

The soldiers have hardly any time for sightseeing in Tripoli; they are ordered by Rommel to the approx. 700km distant front at El Agheila, so we will limit ourselves to only a few impressions of this town. Tripolis, with its Italian architecture.

Für eine Besichtigung von Tripolis blieb den Soldaten kaum Zeit. Sie wurden von Rommel direkt zur etwa 700 km weit entfernten Front bei El Agheila abkommandiert. So beschränken wir uns hier auch auf einige wenige Impressionen dieser Stadt. Das moderne Tripolis mit seiner italienischen Architektur.

"Gazelle" fountains – the cathedral in the background.

Gazellenbrunnen – im Bildhintergrund die Kathedrale.

Catholic cathedral.

Katholische Kathedrale.

The old Arab Tripoli with its Mosques, bazaars and narrow streets.

Das alte arabische Tripolis mit seinen Moscheen, Basars und engen Gassen.

During a break on the way to the front, good photo motifs for the family members back home sometimes turn up.

Während einer Rast auf dem Weg zur Front finden sich manchmal auch lohnenswerte Fotomotive für die Angehörigen daheim.

A "tanker" in a flowerbed between two young palm trees.

Panzersoldat in einem Blumenbeet zwischen jungen Palmen.

Three tank crewmen in front of a palm tree. It is warm, so all are wearing shorts; the two at the front also wear the tropical field cap in the enlisted man's version. The soldier on the left is wearing the ankle-high tropical version of the lace-up shoes, with the socks rolled down to the upper rim of the shaft. The soldier on the right wears the high lace-up boots with shorts, which looks a little odd – but this is war after all, not a fashion show. He carries his tunic rolled up under his arm. He has added a pair of shoulder boards to his shirt. Clearly seen here as well, are the differences in color between the different parts of the uniform, with the uniform of the soldier on the right already looking a bit faded.

3 Panzersoldaten vor einer Palme. Es ist warm, alle tragen Shorts, die beiden vorderen die Tropen-Feldmütze in der Mannschafts-Ausführung. Der linke Soldat trägt die knöchelhohe Tropen-Version der Schnürschuhe, die Socken bis auf den oberen Schaftrand heruntergerollt. Der rechte Soldat die hohen Schnürstiefel zu den Shorts, was etwas seltsam aussieht, aber man ist ja im Krieg und nicht auf einer Modenschau. Seine Feldbluse trägt er zusammengerollt unter dem Arm. Die Schulterklappen hat er an seinem langärmeligen Hemd angebracht. Gut zu sehen sind hier auch Farbunterschiede zwischen den verschiedenen Uniformteilen, wobei die Uniform des rechten Soldaten schon etwas ausgeblichen aussieht.

Soldiers of the *Afrikakorps* with two Arabs. The four soldiers are wearing pith helmets as their head cover. The native peoples in Libya, Egypt and Tunisia were very sympathetic toward the Germans, since the Germans – unlike the Italians, British and French – did not act like Colonial rulers, but instead had a friendly association with them.

4 Soldaten des Afrikakorps mit 2 Arabern. Die 4 Soldaten tragen hier den Tropenhelm als Kopfbedeckung. Die einheimische Bevölkerung in Libyen, Ägypten und Tunesien brachte den deutschen Soldaten viel Sympathie und Unterstützung entgegen, weil die Deutschen entgegen den Italienern, Briten und Franzosen nicht als Kolonialherren auftraten, sondern einen freundlichen Umgang mit ihnen hatten.

Away from civilization one could even take a bath in the Mediterranean. There were strict instructions from the German side not to offend the moral codes of the Muslim natives.

Abseits der Zivilisation konnte auch mal ein Bad im Mittelmeer genommen werden. Von deutscher Seite gab es strikte Anweisungen an die Soldaten, die sittlichen Gefühle der muslimischen Einheimischen nicht zu verletzen.

A tanker on the back deck of the *Panzer* III which we have already become acquainted with, No.521. To the light "service uniform" – consisting of undershirt and shorts – he is wearing the tropical lace shoes. Although rough hobnails were normally affixed to the bottom of the soles in the *Wehrmacht*, the tanker footwear did not have the additional hobnails due to the danger of slipping on the armor plates. He's holding a pith helmet on his knee, a cork hat covered with fabric, with a national colors shield on the right side and a national eagle emblem affixed to the left side. The pith helmet gave its wearer a somewhat picturesque look, but was not popular with the troops since it was quite impractical. The workshop company meanwhile has given the once grey-painted *Panzer* a sand-colored camouflage paint that blends in with the surroundings. At the far right of the picture a steel helmet can be seen that was painted the same color.

Panzersoldat auf dem Heck des uns bereits bekannten Panzers III Nr. 521 sitzend. Zur leichten "Dienstuniform" – aus Unterhemd und Shorts bestehend – trägt er die Tropen-Schnürschuhe. Während normalerweise bei der Wehrmacht unter den Sohlen der Stiefel und Schuhe grobe Stollennägel eingeschlagen wurden, hatte das Schuhwerk der Panzersoldaten wegen der Rutschgefahr auf den Panzerplatten diese zusätzliche Benagelung nicht. Auf dem Knie hält er einen Tropenhelm, ein stoffbezogener Korkhut mit seitlich rechts angebrachtem Nationalfarbenschild und einem Hoheitsadler auf der linken Seite. Der Tropenhelm verlieh seinem Träger zwar ein malerisches Aussehen, bewährte sich aber bei der Truppe nicht, weil er recht unpraktisch war. Der einst grau lackierte Panzer wurde inzwischen von der Werkstatt-Kompanie des Panzer Rgt mit einer der Umgebung angepassten sand-farbigen Tarnlackierung versehen. Ganz rechts im Bild sieht man auch einen Stahlhelm, der mit der gleichen Farbe überlackiert wurde.

Soldiers on the open rear gate of a truck. One has received a field mail package from home. The contents are eagerly inspected – cigarettes, a piece of ham and a sausage. Behind the side one can see two drinking water canisters. Gasoline and water canisters had the same appearance, and so in order to prevent accidental mix-ups, a white cross was painted on both sides of the water canisters.

2 Soldaten auf der geöffneten Heckklappe eines LKW. Einer hat ein Feldpost-Päckchen aus der Heimat enpfangen. Gespannt wird der Inhalt untersucht – Zigaretten, ein Stück Schinken und eine Wurst. Hinter der seitlichen Bordwand sind 2 Trinkwasser-Kanister zu sehen. Die Benzin- und Wasserkanister hatten das gleiche Aussehen. Um Verwechslungen vorzubeugen, war auf den Wasserkanistern beidseitig ein weisses Kreuz aufgemalt.

No tree far and wide, no bush and no toilet. At such times a small hole for human needs was dug somewhere with a spade (in soldier slang, known as going on a "Spading stroll"). Embarrassing only when a comrade snaps your picture in the middle of the activity – at which time only covering one's face is any help.

Weit und breit kein Baum, kein Strauch und keine Toilette. Dann wurde eben irgendwo mit dem Spaten ein kleines Loch für das menschliche Bedürfnis geschaufelt (in der Soldatensprache auch "Spatengang" genannt). Peinlich nur, wenn man dabei von einem Kameraden fotografiert wird, – da hilft nur noch das Gesicht verdecken.

A group of *Afrikakorps* soldiers viewing antique ruins in the vicinity of Naples, Italy. In the background is the smoking volcanic peak of Mt. Vesuvius. Some of the soldiers wear white field caps – the recognition mark of the "Old Boy Africa Vet". New caps and uniforms had an olive green to light brown color shade. Through the effects of sun and washing, these colors faded. Soldier ingenuity also discovered that if Losantin, a chemical contained in the gas decontamination kits, was added to the wash water, it had a strong bleaching effect on textiles. The Africa Vets seen here were probably on a home leave, or recuperation leave and are waiting for the next transport going to Africa.

Eine Gruppe von Soldaten des Afrikakorps bei der Besichtigung antiker Ruinen in der Nähe von Neapel/Italien. Im Hintergrund sieht man den rauchenden Vulkangipfel des Vesuv. Einige der Soldaten tragen weisse Feldmützen – das Erkennungszeichen für "den alten Afrikaner". Neue Feldmützen und Uniformen hatten einen olivgrünen bis hellbraunen Farbton. Durch Sonneneinwirkung und Waschen blichen diese Farben aus. Soldatischer Erfindungsgeist fand dann heraus, dass unter Zugabe des zur Ausrüstung gehörenden Gasentgiftungsmittels Losantin zum Waschwasser, dies eine stark bleichende Wirkung auf Textilien hat. Die hier zu sehenden "alten Afrikaner" waren vermutlich auf Heimat- oder Genesungsurlaub und warten auf den nächsten Transport nach Afrika.

Meeting with a Ju 52 transport aircraft on an airfield. Since there was no harbor for large transport ships along the north African coast at that time besides Tripolis and Tobruk – which were still occupied by the British – the vitally necessary re-supply to the troops of food, field mail, small replacement parts and even fuel was flown by transport aircraft over an increasingly longer supply route from Italy and Sicily, and later from Athens as well as over Crete, to positions behind the front lines. Here the aircrew is taking a brief break, since the engines and canopy are covered with tarps in order to protect them from the effects of sandstorms. In front of the Ju 52 is a *Kübelwagen*. A *swastika* flag is affixed to the front hood, so that from the air, the vehicle can be recognized as German. The vehicle still has the narrow, standard tires – the "*Kübels*"* only received newly developed "balloon" tires during the course of 1942. [* *"Tubs" in soldier slang; this vehicle was the German equivalent of the U.S. Jeep – trans.*]

Begegnung mit einem Transportflugzeug Ju 52 auf einem Feldflugplatz. Da es damals an der nordafrikanischen Mittelmeerküste ausser Tripolis und dem noch von den Briten besetzten Tobruk keine Häfen für grosse Transportschiffe gab, wurde der dringend benötigte Nachschub an Soldaten, Nahrung, Feldpost, kleineren Ersatzteilen und sogar Treibstoff mit zunehmend länger werdenden Nachschubwegen mit Transportflugzeugen direkt von Italien, Sizilien und später auch von Athen über Kreta bis dicht an die Front geflogen. Hier gönnt sich die Flugzeugbesatzung wohl eine Ruhepause, denn die Motoren und die Scheiben des Cockpits sind mit Planen abgedeckt worden, um sie vor den Einwirkungen von Sandstürmen zu schützen. Vor der Ju 52 sieht man einen VW-Kübelwagen. Auf der Fronthaube ist eine Hakenkreuzfahne befestigt, damit dieses Fahrzeug auch aus der Luft als deutsches Fahrzeug erkannt werden kann. Der Kübelwagen hat noch die schmale Standard-Bereifung. Erst im Laufe des Jahres 1942 erhielten die "Kübel" eine neu entwickelte "Ballon"-Bereifung.

A truck column on the way to the front.

LKW Kolonne auf dem Weg zur Front.

Left: A sandstorm nears. Time now to stop the convoy and tightly seal all the doors and canvas tarps on the vehicles. A fine, hot sand will soon darken the sun and make any orientation impossible.

Links: Ein Sandsturm zieht heran. Jetzt wird es Zeit die Fahrzeuge anzuhalten und alle Planen und Türen an den Fahrzeugen dicht zu schliessen. Bald wird der feine heisse Sand die Sonne verdunkeln und eine Orientierung unmöglich machen.

Page 37 left: At the edge of the airfield an NCO waits for the next possibility of transport to the front. He is easily recognizable as a newcomer to Africa by the fresh color of his uniform. The black piping on his shoulderboards identifies his branch (of arms) as combat engineers. Black leather cartridge pouches for [*98K*] rifle ammunition are slid onto his belt. He is reading "*die Oase*" [*The Oasis*], a newspaper put out by the Propaganda company for the German *Afrikakorps*. The headline for the lead article reads, "War as a Creative Power." After imparting its information, the newspaper would be taken along on a "Spading Stroll" instead of toilet paper, which was not available.

Seite 37 links: Am Rande des Feldflughafens wartet ein Uffz. auf die nächste Transportmöglichkeit zur Front. An seiner farbfrischen Uniform ist er als Neuankömmling in Afrika zu erkennen. Die schwarze Umrandung (Paspelierung) seiner Schulterklappen weisst ihn als Angehörigen der Pionier-Truppen aus. Die Sonnen- und Staubschutzbrille hängt um seinem Hals. Am Koppel sind schwarze lederne Patronentaschen für die Karabinermunition aufgeschlauft. Er liest "Die Oase" – eine von der Propagandakompanie herausgegebene Zeitung für das Deutsche Afrikakorps. Die Überschrift des Leitartikels lautet: Krieg als schöpferische Macht. Nach der Informationsvermittlung wurde die Zeitung zum "Spatengang" mitgenommen (anstelle nicht vorhandenem Toilettenpapier).

Page 37 right: A *Panzer* Grenadier [*Armored Infantry soldier*] (recognizable by the light green soutache chevron on his field cap) also reads "*The Oasis*", while sitting on his rucksack. A few *Luftwaffe* soldiers as well as another Army soldier are also visible. In contrast to the Army, the *Luftwaffe* uniform was khaki brown (a more sand-colored shade). As soon as a truck comes by, they will load up their gear and try to get a ride to the vicinity of their unit.

Seite 37 rechts: Ein Panzer-Grenadier (erkennbar an dem hellgrünen Soutachewinkel an der Feldmütze) liest auf seinem Rucksack sitzend ebenfalls "Die Oase". Im Hintergrund sind neben weiteren Heeres-Soldaten auch einige Luftwaffen-Soldaten zu sehen. Im Gegensatz zum Heer, war die Luftwaffen-Uniform khakibraun (ein sandfarbiger Farbton). Sobald ein LKW mit Fahrziel Front vorbeikommt, werden sie ihre Ausrüstung aufladen und versuchen, bis in die Nähe ihrer Einheiten mitgenommen zu werden.

At the city of Benghazi, the street leads through the great El Kuff Wadi. A wadi is a former river valley cut deep into the normal landscape. Near the front, a wadi offered the troops the possibility of good cover from enemy view, however they could also become quite dangerous if it rained in the desert. Since the sand and dust absorb hardly any water, it quickly flows together intpo the depressions and seeks a way toward the sea through the wadis as a raging river. More soldiers drowned in the desert, than died of thirst.

Bei der Stadt Bengasi führt die Strasse durch das grosse Wadi El Kuff. Ein Wadi ist ein tief in das übrige Gelände eingeschnittenes ehemaliges Flusstal. In Frontnähe bot ein Wadi den Truppen gute Deckungsmöglichkeiten vor der Sicht durch den Gegner. Gefährlich konnte es aber werden, wenn es in der Wüste regnete. Da der Sand und Staub kaum das Wasser aufnimmt, fliesst es schnell in den Senken zusammen und sucht sich durch die Wadis als alles mitreissender Fluss einen Weg in Richtung Meer. Es sollen so mehr Soldaten in der Wüste ertrunken sein, als verdurstet.

Impressions from Benghazi. Two shots of the main street. The city of Benghazi is the capitol of the East Libyan province of Cyrenaica and in 1941, had about 65,000 residents. It changed hands five times during the African campaign.

Impressionen aus Benghazi: 2x Hauptstrasse. Die Stadt Benghazi ist die Hauptstadt der ostlibyschen Provinz Cyrenaika und hatte um 1941 etwa 65.000 Einwohner. Während des Afrika-Feldzuges wechselte Bengaszi 5x den Besitzer.

The little city of Dema was well known and loved by the German soldiers due to its good drinking water and oriental flair. View out over the city and the small harbor.

Das Städtchen Derna war bei den Deutschen Soldaten wegen seines guten Trinkwassers und orientalischem Flair bekannt und beliebt. Blick über die Stadt und den kleinen Hafen.

Bazaar in Derna – Germans and Italians as well shop here.

Basar in Derna – auch Deutsche und Italiener kaufen hier ein.

Arab gravesite in Derna.

arabisches Grabmal bei Derna.

A corn dealer astride his donkey.

Maisverkäufer auf seinem Esel.

A carpet dealer.

Teppichhändler.

An Italian woman on a shopping tour at the bazaar.

Italienerinnen beim Einkaufsbummel im Basar.

At Fort Capuzzo, the border dividing Libya and Egypt is passed.

Bei Fort Capuzzo wird der Libyen und Ägypten trennende Grenzzaun passiert.

View from the settlement of Upper Sollum on the high plateau down on Lower Sallum and the Bay of Sallum. From the plateau, a steep road with many curves leads down to the coastal area. All of the vehicular traffic has to pass through this needle's eye. Other units travel uphill in the direction of Libya for rest and refit.

Blick von der auf dem Hochplateau gelegenen Siedlung Ober-Sollum auf Unter-Sollum und die Sollum-Bucht. Vom Plateau führt eine steile kurvenreiche Strasse zur Küstenebene hinunter. Der ganze Verkehr muss durch dieses Nadelöhr. Nachschub rollt bergab zur Front in Ägypten. Andere Verbände fahren zur Erholung und Auffrischung bergauf in Richtung Libyen.

Since the vehicles travelling slowly up and downhill are easy prey for enemy aircraft and bombers, the utmost watchfulness is necessary here. A vehicle with a mounted 20mm antiaircraft gun (*Flak*) is posted at a curve. The flak vehicle is surrounded by a layered stonewall for proctection against weapons fire. The uniforms and the vehicle license plate (*WL = Wehrmacht Luftwaffe*) identify the soldiers as members of the *Luftwaffe* (LW). The gun crew's steel helmets are painted various sand colors, partly matte, partly glossy.

Da die langsam bergauf und -ab fahrenden Fahrzeuge für gegnerische Jagdflugzeuge und Bomber eine leichte Beute darstellen, ist hier höchste Wachsamkeit geboten. In einer Kurve ist ein Fahrzeug mit aufmontierter 2 cm Flugabwehrkanone (Flak) postiert. Als Schutz vor Beschuss ist das Flak-Fahrzeug von aufgeschichteten Steinwällen umgeben. Die Uniformen und das Fahrzeugkennzeichen (WL = Wehrmacht Luftwaffe) weisen die Soldaten als Angehörige der Luftwaffe (LW) aus. Die Stahlhelme der Geschützbedienung sind verschieden sandfarbig lackiert, teilweise matt – teilweise glänzend.

A heavy, half-track prime mover with a towed 88mm *Flak* gun.

Eine schwere Halbketten-Zugmaschine mit angehängtem 8,8 cm Flak-Geschütz.

On the edge of the roadway is another 20mm *Flak* vehicle in position. The gun alertly covers the surrounding area.

Am Rand der Fahrbahn ist ein weiteres 2 cm Flak-Fahrzeug in Stellung. Wachsam sichert das Geschütz nach allen Seiten.

The members of a Propaganda company contemplate the busy street traffic.

Angehörige einer Propaganda-Kompanie betrachten den regen Verkehr auf der Strasse.

This 20mm *Flak* gun has taken position on a hillside.

Dieses 2 cm Flak-Geschütz ist an einem Berghang in Stellung gegangen.

The crew of the truck has gotten off the vehicle to walk, so that the vehicle is lighter in weight and can make it up the incline.

Damit der LKW leichter wird und die Steigung hochkommt, ist die Besatzung abgestiegen und geht zu Fuss.

Left: The well known war correspondent Fritz Moosmüller films the scenery for the Weekly News Report shown back home in theaters.

Links: Der bekannte Kriegsberichterstatter Fritz Moosmüller filmt die Szenerie für die im Kino in der Heimat gezeigten Wochenschau-Berichte.

Page 55 left: Fritz Moosmüller with another photographer from the propaganda company. On the right arm of his tunic he is wearing the "*Afrikakorps*" cufftitle. This cufftitle was introduced, but not generally worn, on 18 July 1941 for all Army troops of the German *Afrikakorps* as a sign of recognition for belonging to this unit. His collar tabs identify him as a Specialist in Officer rank.

Seite 55 links: Fritz Moosmüller mit einem weiteren Fotografen der Propaganda-Kompanie. Am rechten Arm der Feldbluse trägt er den Ärmelstreifen "Afrikakorps". Dieser Ärmelstreifen wurde als Truppenzugehörigkeits-abzeichen am 18. Juni 1941 für alle Heerestruppen des Deutschen Afrikakorps eingeführt – aber nicht generell getragen. Seine Kragenspiegel weisen ihn als Sonderführer im Offiziersrang aus.

Page 55 right: With work completed, Fritz Moosmüller permits himself a pipe. Except for the nearly white field cap, his uniform has a rather medium brown color. Besides the pullover sweater, the pants are conspicuous. At first glance, it looks like he has a pair of *Luftwaffe* pants with the patch pocket mounted on the leg. With this type of trousers, however, the pocket is usually secured with a button visible on the outside. This is probably a case of a privately purchased pair.

Seite 55 rechts: Nach getaner Arbeit gönnt sich Fritz Moosmüller eine Pfeife. Seine Uniform hat bis auf die fast weisse Feldmütze eine eher mittelbraune Farbgebung. Neben dem Pullover fällt hier seine Hose auf. Auf den ersten Blick scheint es sich dabei um eine Luftwaffenhose mit aufgesetzter Beintasche zu handeln. Bei dieser Hose wird die Beintasche jedoch mit einem von aussen sichtbaren Knopf verschlossen. Vermutlich handelt es sich hierbei um eine private Anfertigung vom Schneider.

A Field Police guard – recognizable by his gorget* – directs a vehicle convoy on the way to the Halfaya Pass. [**The gorget worn by military police in the field led to the nickname given them of "chain dogs" – Transl.*]

Ein Posten der Feldgendarmerie – erkennbar an seinem Brustschild – weist eine Fahrzeugkolonne auf den Weg zum Halfaya-Pass ein.

The Mosque in Unter-Sollum, destroyed in the fighting.

Die durch Kriegseinwirkungen zerstörte Moschee in Unter-Sollum.

A German soldier in a terrain consultation with two Arabs.

Ein Deutscher Soldat bei einer Geländebesprechung mit zwei Arabern.

The street leading to Marsa Matruk.This area and its surroundings were wrested from the British troops on June 28, 1942, after a bitter defense. Over 6000 British prisoners were taken into German captivity here.

Strasse nach Marsa Matruk. Dieser Ort und seine Umgebung wurde am 28. Juni 1942 nach erbitterter Gegenwehr den Britischen Truppen abgerungen. Über 6.000 Briten gerieten hier in Deutsche Gefangenschaft.

Protective trenches laid in front of Marsa Matruk by the British.

Von den Briten angelegte Schützengräben vor Marsa Matruk.

An Italian M13/40 tank before Marsa Matruk.

Italienischer Panzer M13/40 vor Marsa Matruk.

An Italian truck before Marsa Matruk.

Italienischer LKW vor Marsa Matruk.

A shipwreck in the harbor of Marsa Matruk.

Schiffswrack im Hafen von Marsa Matruk.

An 88mm *Flak* gun position on the coast near Marsa Matruk.

8,8 cm Flak – Stellungen an der Küste bei Marsa Matruk.

Decoy Flak position at the edge of an airfield. A destroyed Bofors (?) gun is set up in such a manner that it looks intact from a distance. Straw dummies equipped with worn out uniforms and pith helmets complete the bluff.

Flak-Scheinstellung am Rande eines Feldflughafens. Ein zerstörtes Flak-Geschütz (Bofors ?) ist so aufgebaut worden, dass es von weitem intakt aussieht. Mit ausgedienten Uniformen und Tropenhelmen versehene Strohpuppen vervollständigen den Bluff.

The soldiers have put a lot of space between their tents, so as not to offer the enemy airforce a rewarding target. *Die Soldaten haben ihre Zelte weit verteilt, um der gegnerischen Luftwaffe keine lohnenden Ziele zu bieten.*

A soldier with a shouldered spade – probably just returning from a "spading stroll".

Soldat mit geschultertem Spaten, vermutlich kommt er vom "Spatengang".

In the background one can see the "white" mosque at Sidi Abd El Rahman, a building visible from afar, where the German attack was finally brought to a standstill. Only a few kilometers south of this mosque lies the spot where, on September 30, 1942, the highly decorated fighter pilot Hans-Joachim Marseille bailed out of his Me 109 aircraft due to engine trouble. As he jumped, however, he struck the aircraft tail and fell to his death with an unopened parachute.

Im Hintergrund sieht man "die weisse Moschee" bei Sidi Abd El Rahman. Ein weithin sichtbares Gebäude nahe El Alamein, wo der Deutsche Angriff endgültig zum Stehen gebracht wurde. Nur wenige Kilometer südlich dieser Moschee liegt die Stelle, wo am 30. September 1942 der hochdekorierte Jagdflieger Hans-Joachim Marseille auf Grund eines Maschinenschadens seines Me 109 Jagdflugzeugs mit dem Fallschirm aussteigen wollte. Beim Absprung prallte er jedoch an das Leitwerk und fiel mit ungeöffnetem Fallschirm in den Tod.

Flak troops bring their 88mm gun into position. The heavy 18 ton "*Famo*"* towing vehicle has driven the gun on its chassis (limber) into a prepared covered depression. After removal of the two-piece limber, the spreader spars are deployed so that the gun has a sturdy base. The crew belong to the *Luftwaffe* anti-aircraft artillery (*Flak*) branch and wear the usual uniform with garrison cap. Only the soldier to the left of the towing vehicle is wearing an Army style field cap. Since at this time the *Luftwaffe* was not officially equipped with this type of cap, it may be either a private purchase example or a "loaner" from the Army. [*See glossary under "Vehicles" – Transl.*]

Flak-Soldaten bringen ihr 8,8 cm Geschütz in Stellung. Die schwere 18 to. Famo-Zugmaschine hat das Geschütz mit seinem Fahrwerk (Protze) in ein vorbereitetes Deckungsloch gefahren. Nach Entfernen der zweiteiligen Protze werden die Spreizholme ausgeklappt, damit das Geschützt einen sicheren Stand hat. Die Bedienungsmannschaft gehört zur Luftwaffen Flak und trägt auch deren typische Uniform mit der Schiffchenmütze. Nur der Soldat links auf der Zugmaschine trägt eine Feldmütze im Heeresstil. Da die Luftwaffe zu diesem Zeitpunkt offiziell noch nicht über diesen Mützentyp verfügte, kann es sich hierbei nur um eine Privatanfertigung oder eine "Leihgabe" vom Heer handeln.

The *Flak* gunners prepare ammunition. For reasons of security, munitions were transported without fuses, which are now screwed onto the top [*of the shells*]. The *Flak* 88 was actually an anti-aircraft gun, which proved itself during the war however, as a highly precise and effective anti-tank weapon. At Tobruk, a British destroyer was sunk by an 88 gun battery (normally four guns). For ground fighting [*direct fire – Transl.*] this gun was refitted with an added steel shield to give the gunners behind it some protection from small arrms fire. In the pictures, the Luftwaffe tropical pants with the leg pouch pocket are easy to recognize. In addition, there are two types of pullover, one with a "V"-shaped neck opening and one with a roll-neck collar.

Die Flak-Kanoniere bereiten neben der 8.8 die Munition vor. Die Munition wurde aus Sicherheitsgründen ohne Zünder transportiert, welche hier jetzt aufgeschraubt werden. Die 8.8 Flak war eigentlich ein Flugabwehrgeschütz, welches sich aber im 2. Weltkrieg auch als höchst präzise und wirkungsvolle Panzerabwehrwaffe bewährte. Bei Tobruk wurde von einer 8.8 Batterie (das sind in der Regel 4 Geschütze) ein britischer Zerstörer versenkt. Für den Bodenkampf ist dieses Geschütz mit einem zusätzlichen Stahlschild nachgerüstet worden, um den Kanonieren dahinter Schutz gegen Beschuss durch leichte Waffen zu geben. Auf den Fotos ist die LW-Tropenhose mit der aufgesetzten Beintasche gut zu erkennen. Desweiteren zwei verschiedene Typen von Pullovern, einmal mit V-förmigen Halsausschnitt und einmal mit Rollkragen.

The cameraman from the propaganda company is instructed in the operation of the *Flak* battery's rangefinder (four meter base) by a Sergeant. The data is transmitted from the rangefinder by underground cable through the Auxiliary command device to the individual guns. The Sergeant is wearing blue [*continental*] shoulderboards on his shirt and two *Luftwaffe* soldiers in the background are wearing the blue garrison cap.* [**A boat shaped cap, in Luftwaffe terminology called a "Fliegermütze" – Transl.*]

Der Kameramann von der Propaganda-Kompanie lässt sich von einem Unteroffizier das zu der Flak-Batterie gehörende Entfernungs-Messgerät (4 Meter Basis) erklären. Vom Entfernungs-Messgerät wurden die ermittelten Daten per Kabel über das Kommando-Hilfsgerät an die einzelnen Geschütze weitergeleitet. Der Uffz. trägt an seinem Hemd blaue Schulterklappen und zwei LW-Soldaten im Hintergrund blaue Schiffchenmützen.

An 88mm gun in a night firefight.

8.8 Geschütze im nächtlichen Feuergefecht.

Columns of smoke visible from afar point the way to the victims of this 88mm gun.

Weithin sichtbare Rauchsäulen weisen den Weg zu den Opfern der 8.8.

A British aircraft has crashed and burned on the ground, It is possible to determine the aircraft is British only from the engine block and pieces of the remaining fuselage with the tri-color national emblem.

Ein britisches Flugzeug ist am Boden zerschellt und ausgebrannt. Nur vom Motorblock und einem Stück der Rumpfverkleidung mit dem 3-farbigen Nationalitätsabzeichen kann man noch auf ein britisches Flugzeug schliessen.

Pieces of wreckage from British Wellington bombers line the route.

Wrackteile von britischen Wellington Bombern säumen den Weg.

A *Panzer* III with long bore 50mm cannon, at full speed. It leaves a dust cloud behind it that blocks the photographer's view.

Ein Panzer III mit 5 cm Langrohrkanone in voller Fahrt. Hinter sich lässt er eine Staubwolke, die dem Fotografen die Sicht nimmt.

A *Panzer* III carries travelling companions to the front.

Ein Panzer III nimmt Fahrgäste mit zur Front.

August 29, 1942. Movement into the assembly area positions for the Second Battle of El Alamein (the so called "six-day race").

29. August 1942 Aufmarsch in den Bereitstellungsräumen zur 2. Alamein -Schlacht (dem sogenannten "6 Tage Rennen").

An antitank crew brings their 75mm antitank gun (*PaK*) into position. The uniform coloring shows a lot of variety, from sandy beige to olive green.

Panzerjäger bringen ihre 7,5 cm Panzerabwehrkanone (PaK) in Stellung. Die Farbgebung der Uniformen ist sehr vielfältig – von sandbeige bis olivgrün.

Antitank gun at the moment of firing – this may be a modified, captured Russian 76.2mm, which were employed in large numbers by the troops in North Africa. A number of shell casings already lie around in the picture foreground.

PaK beim Abschuss – hierbei könnte es sich um ein umgebautes russisches 7,62 cm Beutegeschütz handeln, welche in Nordafrika in grösseren Stückzahlen bei der Truppe eingesetzt wurden. Im Bildvordergrund liegen bereits etliche leere Geschosshülsen.

For these British soldiers the war is over. They are brought to a POW camp behind the front lines by a German escort. The German guard preceding the column carries his steel helmet, covered with a sackcloth camouflage cover, hanging from his arm.

Für diese britischen Soldaten ist der Krieg zu Ende. Von einer deutschen Eskorte werden sie hinter die Front in ein Gefangenenlager gebracht. Der vorn gehende deutsche Bewacher trägt seinen mit einem Sackleinen-Tarnüberzug versehenen Stahlhelm am Arm.

On the occasion of the burial of fallen comrades, high-ranking officers arrive at the cemetary. In the front, *General* Schnarrenberger; he wears a tailored tropical field tunic with general's collar tabs, and the "*Afrikakorps*" cufftitle [sleeveband], a pair of breeches with red [*general's*] side stripes, high-necked leather boots and a field cap with gold piping. On his right breast pocket he wears the German Cross in Gold. In the center of the picture is the Commander of *Panzer* Regiment 5, Colonel Gerhard Müller. In the French campaign he was awarded the 1939 *Spange** [*clasp*] to the Iron Cross 1st and 2nd Class, both of which he had won previously during World War I.; the *Spange* represented a second, post 1939 award of these decorations. Although he had lost his left arm in September of 1941 in the heavy fighting in Russia, he got himself transferred back to the combat troops as soon as he had recovered. In Africa, he had led *Panzer* Regiment 5 personally from the front line in over sixty *Panzer* attacks since 1 February. He was awarded the Knights Cross to the Iron Cross for this on September 9, 1942. He was jokingly named "*Panzer*-Müller", or "The Old Man" by his soldiers. His unconventional style is also mirrored in his uniform. He wears a pair of *Luftwaffe* trousers with the exterior pouch pocket, and an officer's visor cap together with his field tunic with the *Panzer* Death's Head insignia on the collar lapels. In the background is a 2nd Lieutenant with a black *Panzer* overseas cap. To the right stands an officer with the tropical, webbed version of the officer's belt with a round buckle. [**The Spange is the silver eagle on the ribbon at the second button, and above the Iron Cross 1st Class on the pocket. See the Glossary under "Awards"– Transl.*]

Anlässlich der Beerdigung von gefallenen Kameraden haben sich ranghohe Offiziere auf dem Friedhof eingefunden. Vorn Generalmajor Schnarrenberger, er trägt zu seiner vom Schneider stammenden Tropen-Feldbluse mit den Generals-Kragenspiegeln und Afrikakorps-Ärmelband, eine Breecheshose mit roten Seitenstreifen, lederne Schaftstiefel und eine Feldmütze mit goldfarbigen Vorstössen. An der rechten Brusttasche trägt er das "Deutsche Kreuz in Gold". In der Bildmitte ist der Kommandeur des Pz Rgt 5 Oberst Gerhard Müller zu sehen. Im Frankreich-Feldzug wurden ihm bereits die Wiederholungsspangen zum Eisernen Kreuz 2. und 1. Klasse verliehen. Obwohl er im September 1941 bei den schweren Kämpfen in Russland seinen linken Arm verloren hatte, liess er sich nach seiner Genesung wieder zur kämpfenden Truppe versetzen. Seit Februar 1942 führte er das Pz Rgt 5 in Afrika persönlich in vorderster Front in 60 Panzerangriffen. Dafür wurde ihm am 9. September 1942 das Ritterkreuz des Eisernen Kreuzes verliehen. Von seinen Soldaten wurde er scherzhaft "Panzer-Müller" oder "Der Alte" genannt. Seine unkonventionelle Art spiegelt sich auch in seiner Uniform wieder. Zur Feldbluse mit den Panzer-Totenköpfen am Kragen, trägt er eine LW- Hose mit aufgesetzter Beintasche und eine Offiziers-Schirmmütze. Im Hintergrund links ist ein Leutnant mit schwarzer Panzer-Schiffchen-Mütze zu sehen. Rechts steht ein Offizier mit der Tropenausführung der Offiziers-Feldbinde mit dem runden Koppelschloss am Webstoff-Riemen.

General Schnarrenberger lays a large flower-decorated wreath on the graves of the dead. In view of the high-ranking funeral guests and the large wreath, it could hardly be simple soldiers being interred here.

General Schnarrenberger legt grosse blumengeschmückte Kränze an den Gräbern der Gefallenen nieder. Angesichts der hochrangingen Trauergäste und der grossen Kränze wurden hier wohl keine einfachen Soldaten beerdigt.

A military chaplain carries out the ceremony. He wears the Army tropical uniform, but without any shoulderboards. Besides the already named officers, a military band and the comrades of the fallen (with helmets) also take part in the ceremony as an Honor Guard.

Ein Militär-Pfarrer vollzieht die Trauerfeier. Er trägt die Tropen-Uniform des Heeres, jedoch ohne Schulterklappen. Neben den zuvor genannten Offizieren nehmen auch Kameraden der Gefallenen, ein Ehrenzug (mit Stahlhelmen) und eine Militärkapelle an der Trauerfeier teil.

The grave of *Generalleutnant*[*] Georg von Bismark, who was mortally wounded in an air attack on August 31, 1942 during the 2nd El Alamein battle while leading from the spearhead of the 21st *Panzer* Division, which he commanded. For sentimental feelings, however, this was the wrong place – the battle of El Alamein raged relentlessly onward. [[*]*Major General*]

Das Grabmal von Generalleutnant Georg von Bismarck, der am 31. August 1942 während der 2. Alamein Schlacht an der Spitze der von ihm befehligten 21. Panzerdivision durch einen Luftangriff tödlich verwundet wurde. Aber für sentimentale Gefühle war hier der falsche Platz – die Schlacht um El Alamein tobte unerbittlich weiter.

Left: The gunner of a heavy Artillery piece has sighted a new target through his gun optics [*gunsight*]. Behind him, the gun commander calculates the tube elevation and powder charge necessary for the desired trajectory.

Links: Der Richtschütze eines schweren Artilleriegeschützes hat mit der Geschützoptik ein neues Ziel anvisiert. Hinter ihm berechnet der Geschützführer die für die Geschossbahn nötige Rohrneigung und Treibladungsmenge.

Right: A 210mm long-bore gun at the moment the round is fired. A cloud of smoke is distinctly visble leaving the end of the guntube. The cannoneers hold their ears closed, to avoid damage to their hearing. These guns were the heaviest caliber weapon in use on the German side in North Africa.

Rechts: Ein 21 cm Langrohrgeschütz bei der Schussabgabe. Deutlich sichtbar verlässt eine Pulverwolke das Rohr. Die Kanoniere halten sich die Ohren zu, damit ihr Gehör keinen Schaden nimmt. Diese Geschütze waren auf deutscher Seite die schwersten in Nordafrika eingesetzten Waffen.

The loader removes the still smoking propellant cartridge case from the breech. In order to prevent his hands from being burned, he wears heat-resistant gloves. The red soutache of the Artillery branch is clearly visible on his field cap.

Der Ladeschütze entnimmt die noch qualmende Treibladungshülse aus dem Verschluss. Um sich seine Hände nicht zu verbrennen trägt er hitzebeständige Handschuhe. An seiner Feldmütze ist deutlich der Rote Soutache-Winkel der Artilleristen zu erkennen.

So as not to present a target of its own, visible from a considerable distance, the gun tube is lowered again.

Das Geschützrohr ist wieder abgesenkt worden, um nicht selbst als weithin sichtbares Ziel zu dienen.

Antitank soldiers have dug out a large, round depression for their 75mm *PaK* gun so that in the level terrain the gun itself offers a minimal surface for attack, yet can still be turned to all sides in this depression. In addition, the gun shield is camoflaged with a sand-colored tarp. At the front left lies a spread out camouflage net that can be quickly pulled up over the gun during attacks by enemy aircraft. The gunner has sighted a target.

Panzerjäger haben für ihre 7,5 cm PaK eine grosse runde Vertiefung ausgehoben, damit das Geschütz in der Ebene selbst nur eine geringe Angriffsfläche bietet und in dieser Vertiefung auch nach allen Seiten gedreht werden kann. Zusätzlich wurde das Schutzschild mit einer sandfarbigen Plane getarnt. Vorne links liegt auch noch ein ausgebreitetes Tarnnetz, welches bei Angriffen durch gegnerische Flieger schnell über die Geschützstellung gezogen werden konnte. Der Richtschütze hat ein Ziel anvisiert.

Two German soldiers in their foxholes during a break in the fighting. Due to the rocky ground, they haven't been able to dig in and so have built up some cover with sandbags. The soldier in front is wearing a mosquito net over his field cap. This fine mesh, greenish mosquito net was an official item of *Wehrmacht* equipment and was issued to soldiers in the tropics and in Russia. A few other items are also visible: helmet, map case, drinking cups from the canteen, a food packet and a tin can (canned meat?).

Zwei deutsche Infanteristen während einer Gefechtspause in ihrem Deckungsloch. Wegen des felsigen Bodens haben sie sich nicht eingraben können und deshalb mit Sandsäcken eine Deckung aufgebaut. Der vordere Soldat trägt einen Mückenschleier über seiner Feldmütze. Dieser feinmaschige grünliche Mückenschleier war ein offizielles Ausrüstungsteil der Wehrmacht und wurde an Soldaten in den Tropen und in den Sumpfgebieten Russlands ausgegeben. Neben dem Schutz des Kopfes vor Mücken und Fliegen wurde er auch als Tarnüberzug verwandt. Es sind auch einige Ausrüstungsteile zu sehen: Stahlhelm, Kartentasche, Trinkbecher von Feldflaschen, Verpflegungspäckchen und eine Dose (Büchsenfleisch?).

A group of soldiers during construction of a command bunker. Over a hole in the rocky ground, they lay railroad ties, which will support the covering. The personal I.D.* with the leather chest pouch, is visible on the man with the bare torso. The soldier in the left corner of the picture is wearing what appears to be a body winding-wrap, partly hidden by the his trousers. In accordance with an official regulation, this body winding-wrap was to be worn during the night and during the cooler parts of the date as protection from colds, and abdominal inflammation. [*A metal disk stamped on both sides, roughly equivalent to the U.S. "Dogtag" – Transl.]

Eine Gruppe Soldaten beim Bau eines Behelfsbunkers. Über ein Loch in dem felsigen Boden legen sie Eisenbahnschienen, die die Abdeckung tragen sollen. Bei dem stehenden Soldaten mit nacktem Oberkörper sieht man seine Erkennungsmarke mit dem ledernen Brustbeutel. Der Soldat am linken Bildrand trägt anscheinend eine, zum Teil von der Hose verdeckte, Leibbinde (Nierenschutz).Gemäss einer Dienstanweisung war diese Leibbinde während der Nacht und den kühleren Tageszeiten zum Schutz vor Erkältungen und Unterleibsentzündungen zu tragen.

These two soldiers have found a valuable commodity in a deserted British position – a barrel with drinking water. After having already filled their twenty liter* drinking-water cans, the rest is transferred to empty Italian wine bottles. On the Alamein Front, drinking water was at times in such short supply that only one liter per man per day could be distributed. The water had to be brought over great distances. There were special units, of course, that drilled wells and de-salinated seawater, but these could not even come close to covering the huge water requirement. For personal hygiene and for laundry, seawater or salty well water were used, when available. The soldier on the right also wears a body winding-wrap – and gym shoes! [*About 5.2 U.S. gallons – Transl.*]

Diese beiden Soldaten haben in einer aufgegebenen britischen Stellung ein kostbares Gut gefunden – eine Tonne mit Trinkwasser. Nachdem sie ihren 20 Liter Trinkwasserkanister bereits aufgefüllt haben, wird der Rest in leere italienische Weinflaschen umgefüllt. An der Alamein-Front war auf deutscher Seite das Trinkwasser teilweise so knapp, dass pro Mann und Tag nur 1 Liter ausgegeben werden konnte. Das Wasser musste über weite Entfernungen herangeschafft werden. Es gab zwar spezielle Einheiten die Brunnen bohrten und Meerwasser-Entsalzungsanlagen, aber die konnten den riesigen Wasserbedarf auch nicht ausreichend decken. Für die Körperpflege und zum Waschen der Wäsche wurde, insofern überhaupt vorhanden, Meerwasser oder salziges Brunnenwasser genommen. Der rechte Soldat trägt hier wohl ebenfalls eine Leibbinde und weisse Turnschuhe !

Another German soldier has had success amongst the items left behind by the British. In front of the wooden crate stands a tin canister with the label "WATER". Field Marshal Rommel once said to his officers: "If the British sink the ships with our supplies, then we'll take our supplies from the British."

Ein weiterer deutscher Soldat ist in den Hinterlassenschaften der Briten fündig geworden. Vor den Holzkisten steht ein Blechkanister mit der Aufschrift "WATER". Feldmarschall Rommel sagte einmal zu seinen Offizieren: " Wenn die Briten unsere Schiffe mit dem Nachschub versenken, dann holen wir uns den Nachschub von den Briten".

Two sergeants from the propaganda company enjoy a warm meal from the field kitchen – in soldier's terminology nicknamed the "Gulash cannon" (in the right background). Instead of plates they are eating out of large, empty preserve cans. The sergeant farthest left wears a standard field tunic with the sewn on brownish collar tabs for NCO ranks. These tabs are missing from the tunic collar of the sergeant on the right. There is no soutache on either field cap; for reasons of standardization, no further caps were manufactured with a soutache after the middle of 1942, and the soutache chevron was to be removed from caps that had one – a rule which was not generally followed.

Zwei Feldwebel von der Propaganda-Kompanie geniessen eine warme Mahlzeit aus der Feldküche – in der Soldatensprache auch "Gulaschkanone" genannt – rechts im Hintergrund. Anstelle von Tellern wird hier aus grossen leeren Konservendosen gegessen. Der Fotoapparat liegt solange auf dem Essensträger (vorne links) ein Warmhaltebehälter, der wie ein Rucksack getragen wurde und mit dem das Essen zu den Soldaten in der vorderen Front gebracht wurde. Der linke Feldwebel trägt eine Standard-Feldbluse, mit der ab dem Unteroffiziers-Dienstrang um den Kragen aufgenähten bräunlichen Litze. An der Feldbluse des rechten Feldwebels fehlt diese Kragenlitze. An beiden Feldmützen ist kein Soutache-Winkel in der Waffenfarbe zu sehen. Aus Gründen der Vereinheitlichung wurden ab Mitte 1942 keine Feldmützen mehr mit Soutache-Winkel hergestellt und bei den vorhandenen sollte der Soutachewinkel entfernt werden, was aber nicht generell befolgt wurde.

Field cooks at work. Noodles are formed by hand and then cooked in a cauldron made from a halved gas cannister.

Feldköche bei der Arbeit. Mit der Hand werden Knödel geformt und dann in einem zum Kochkessel umfunktionierten halbierten Benzinfass gekocht.

Left: *Major* Jäckel also enjoys a meal from a can. His eating utensils are a "*Göffel*" – a knife, fork, and spoon set that could be secured together – with a *Gabel* (fork) on one side, and a *Löffel* (spoon) on the other. *Major* Jäckel is wearing a tunic with enlisted man's collar tabs. On his left breast pocket is the Rider's Achievement Badge, definite evidence that he was originally a Cavalryman. He is also wearing an Iron Cross 2nd Class ribbon slipped through a buttonhole and also a blue ribbon, which may belong to the *Wehrmacht* service award.* There was no special food for German officers, it was the same for all ranks. This was quite different among the Italian comrades in arms, where there were three different categories of meals: Enlisted Men, NCO, Officer. [**Long-service, first awarded upon completion of 4 years of unbroken service, and then in increments thereafter. – Transl.*]

Links: Auch Major Jäckel geniesst die Mahlzeit aus der Blechdose. Sein Essbesteck ist ein "Göffel" – das ist ein in der mitte zusammenklappbares Essbesteck, auf der einen Seite eine ***G****abel und auf der anderen Seite ein* ***Lö****ffel. Major Jäckel trägt eine Feldbluse mit Mannschaftskragenspiegel. Auf der linken Brusttasche sieht man das Reiter-Leistungsabzeichen, ein sicheres Indiz, dass er ursprünglich ein Kavallerist war. Desweiteren trägt er das durch ein Knopfloch geschlaufte Ordensband vom EK 2 und ein blaues Band, welches zu der Wehrmachts-Dienstauszeichnung gehören könnte. Bei den deutschen Soldaten gab es keine besondere Kost für die Offiziere, sie war für alle Dienstränge gleich. Bei den italienischen Waffenbrüdern sah das ganz anders aus, dort gab es 3 verschiedene Küchen-Kategorien: Mannschaften, Unteroffiziere, Offiziere.*

Opposite: This artilleryman indulges in a meal of canned meat. The Italian canned meat was little loved by the Africa soldiers. These cans bear the stamp "AM". The German soldiers named this "old boy", or "old hinny."* [**The first letters of the German words thus abbreviate as "AM" in either case; a "hinny' is the issue of a male horse, and a female donkey – transl*].

*Nächste Seite: Dieser Artillerist gönnt sich eine Dose Büchsenfleisch. Wenig beliebt war bei den Afrikakämpfern das italienische Büchsenfleisch. Diese Dosen trugen den Stempelaufdruck "AM". Von den deutschen Soldaten "****A****lter* ***M****ann" oder "****A****ltes* ***M****uli" genannt.*

Is this signals soldier a newcomer to Africa? His pale skin and brightly colored field cap with the light yellow soutache chevron suggests this is the case. He hasn't grown accustomed to the sparse food yet – he suspiciously sorts through the rice on his plate with his fingers. Could there be something still alive crawling around in there?

Ob dieser Soldat der Nachrichtentruppe wohl noch neu in Afrika ist ? Seine blasse Haut und farbfrische Feldmütze mit dem hellgelben Soutachewinkel lassen dies vermuten. An die karge Kost hat er sich noch nicht gewöhnt – misstrauisch sortiert er mit seinen Fingern den Reis auf seinem Teller. Ob da wohl noch was lebendiges zwischen rumkrabbelt?

The company tailor, who is responsible for the repair or adjustment of his comrades' uniforms, has temporarily put aside needle and thread and is writing a letter home to his family on the sewing machine table. He may have sewn his own uniform tunic since it is made of the brownish wool felt from which overcoats were produced. The national eagle emblem also does not correspond to the color pattern of the tropical version. A private's chevron is sewn on the left sleeve.

Der Kompanie-Schneider, der für die feldmässige Reparatur oder Änderung der Uniformen seiner Kameraden zuständig ist, hat Nadel und Faden erst einmal zur Seite gelegt und schreibt am Nähmaschinentischchen einen Feldpostbrief an seine Familie. Seine Uniformjacke könnte er sich selbst genäht haben, denn sie besteht anscheinend aus dem bräunlichen Wollfilz aus dem die Mäntel gefertigt wurden. Der Hoheitsadler entspricht in der Farbgebung auch nicht dem Tropen-Hoheitsadler. Auf dem linken Ärmel ist ein Gefreitenwinkel angebracht.

On a scouting mission with the VW *Kübelwagen*, built on the chasis of the VW-Beetle. With the large balloon tires introduced in 1942, it mastered almost any terrain.

Mit dem auf der Basis des VW-Käfers gebauten VW-Kübelwagen auf Erkundungsfahrt in der Wüste. Mit den 1942 eingeführten grossen Ballonreifen meisterte er fast jedes Gelände.

WH-936769

Diverse is the face of the desert. Not only endless sand dunes, but also flat areas overlaid with fine gravel, or depressions with a light growth of shrubbery give the desert an ascerbic beauty, which for their entire lives, the Africa soldiers will never forget.

Vielfältig ist das Gesicht der Wüste. Nicht nur endlose Sanddünen, auch Felswüsten, mit feinem Schotter überzogene Flächen, oder Senken mit leichtem Strauchbewuchs, geben der Wüste eine herbe Schönheit, die die Afrikakämpfer zeitlebens nicht vergessen.

Right: View out of a truck cab toward a "tent village" in a rear area. At the front left is a field hospital, constructed of several tents assembled together, which is marked with a Red Cross flag. The British Major Sam Bradshaw, with severe wounds, was delivered to a German field hospital in the fall of 1942 at El Alamein. He said at one time: "I lay there with German, Italian and my own comrades – from simple soldiers to officers. We all received the same degree of medical care and attention from the German doctors and nurses. Although we were bitter opponents on the battlefield, this animosity was not carried over to the wounded or to prisoners. And so it was on both sides of the front lines, and that was the extraordinary thing about the African campaign."

Recht: Blick aus einem LKW-Führerhaus auf ein Zeltdorf im rückwärtigen Kampfgebiet. Vorne links sieht man ein aus mehreren Zelten zusammengefügtes Feldlazarett, welches mit einer Rot-Kreuz Fahne gekennzeichnet ist. Der Britische Major Sam Bradshaw wurde im Herbst 1942 bei El Alamein mit schweren Verwundungen in ein deutsches Feldlazarett eingeliefert. Er sagte einmal: "Ich habe dort mit Deutschen, Italienern und eigenen Kameraden gelegen – vom einfachen Soldaten bis zum Offizier. Von den deutschen Medizinern und Krankenschwestern haben wir alle die gleiche medizinische Betreuung und Pflege erfahren. Obwohl wir auf dem Schlachtfeld erbitterte Gegner waren, so wurde diese Feindseligkeit nicht auf verwundete oder gefangene Gegner übertragen. So war es auf beiden Seiten der Front und das war das Besondere am Afrika-Feldzug".

A short rest stop is used to orient oneself using a map and compass.

Eine kurze Rast wird genutzt um sich mittels Karte und Kompass zu orientieren.

A little time remains for reading the "illustrated"* papers that were sent along with the field mail from home. [*Tabloid style – Transl.]

Zum Lesen der mit der Feldpost aus der Heimat zugesandten Illustrierten bleibt auch noch etwas Zeit.

Deutsche Illustrierte
DIE WOCHE

The sun is already quite low on the horizon – time to search out a spot for the night.

Die Sonne steht schon recht tief am Horizont – Zeit um sich einen Platz für die Nacht zu suchen.

In a depression with a lush growth of brush, one comes across a unit that has hidden itself here quite skillfully against being spotted by the eyes of enemy pilots that may chance by. Other than the truck, it is hard to see that an entire "tent village" is hidden here.

In einer Senke mit recht üppigem Strauchbewuchs trifft man auf eine Einheit, die sich hier recht geschickt vor den Augen zufällig vorbeikommender gegnerischer Flieger versteckt hat. Ausser dem LKW sieht man hier kaum, dass hier ein ganzes Zeltdorf versteckt wurde.

In a depression, protected from the cold night wind, they have found a suitable place. The war correspondents have also slept much better on the field cots that they brought with them than their comrades among the combat troops in foxholes at the front. The photographer has already awakened and holds his companions frozen in a picture. While those behind the *Kübel* can't decide yet whether or not to get up, the one in the front is already putting on his shoes. He has, of course, already checked them to make sure that no scorpion, or even a sandviper, has taken up quarters inside overnight. It looks like he already needs new socks again, since the big toe is showing through these.

In einer Senke, geschützt vor dem nächtlichen kalten Wind hatten sie einen passenden Platz gefunden. Auf den mitgenommenen Feldbetten haben die Kriegsberichterstatter auch wesentlich besser geschlafen als die Kameraden von der kämpfenden Truppe im Deckungsloch an der Front. Der Fotograf ist bereits aufgestanden und hält seine Begleiter im Bild fest. Während der hinter dem Kübel liegende sich noch nicht entschliessen kann aufzustehen, zieht sich der vordere schon seine Schuhe an. Natürlich hat er sich vorher vergewissert, dass sich darin kein Skorpion oder gar eine Sandviper über Nacht einquartiert hat. Neue Socken bräuchte er auch mal wieder, denn bei diesen schaut schon der grosse Zeh hinaus.

After a little rain shower, one experiences a spectacle of Nature rare in the desert: a rainbow is faintly visible on the horizon.

Nach einem kleinen Regenschauer erlebt man ein in der Wüste eher seltenes Naturschauspiel. Ein Regenbogen ist schwach am Horizont zu sehen.

A group shot with comrades and a VW-*Kübel*. The soldier on the right is wearing his newly awarded Iron Cross 2nd Class, which was affixed to the buttonhole of his field tunic during the award ceremony. He will take the award off later and send it home with the field mail, and then wear only the award ribbon in the upper buttonhole, like his comrade in the center of the picture. Of particular note in this picture is the insignia on the front of the *Kübelwagen's* mudguard, which shows a winged camel with the letters "*PK*" for *Propaganda Kompanie* [Propaganda Company].

Gruppenbild mit Kameraden und VW-Kübel. Der rechte Soldat trägt noch sein ihm frisch verliehenes EK 2, welches ihm bei der Verleihung durch ein Knopfloch seiner Feldbluse angeheftet wurde. Später wird er den Orden abnehmen und mit der Feldpost nach Hause schicken. Dann trägt er auch nur noch ein Stück des Ordensbandes im oberen Knopfloch wie sein Kamerad in der Bildmitte. Besonders zu beachten ist auf diesem Foto das auf dem vorderen Schutzblech des Kübels angebrachte Abzeichen. Es zeigt ein geflügeltes Kamel mit den Buchstaben PK = Propaganda-Kompanie.

Chance meetings with Beduines as a rule were usually very friendly despite language problems. That one could do a good trade business with the Germans had been passed around until it reached every last Bedouin tent. The dark skinned fellow with the Fez wears what appears to be a German tunic. It could be that like many of his fellow countrymen, he worked as an auxiliary helper for the Germans.

Zufällige Begegnungen mit Beduinen fielen in der Regel trotz Sprachproblemen sehr freundlich aus. Dass man mit den Deutschen gute Tauschgeschäfte tätigen konnte, hatte sich bis in das letzte Beduinenzelt herumgesprochen. Der dunkelhäutige mit dem Fez trägt anscheinend eine deutsche Feldbluse. Es kann sein, dass er wie viele andere seiner Landsleute, als Hilfskraft für die Deutschen arbeitete.

Italian soldiers exhausted from battle, rest against the corner of a building. Between them are two Beduines. The one at the front is already fitted out with German tropical shoes.

Vom Kampf erschöpfte italienische Soldaten ruhen sich an einer Gebäudeecke aus. Dazwischen sind zwei Beduinen zu sehen, wovon der vordere bereits mit deutschen Tropen-Schuhen ausgestattet ist.

Following is an excerpt from the diary of *Obergefreiter [Corporal]* Hans Hesse, who came to *Panzer* Grenadier Rgt. 433 (164th Light Africa Division) in North Africa in the middle of July 1942:

> "Combat area El Alamein: with pickaxe and shovel our platoon has built up a hedgehog position (an all-round defensive position) from the stony earth. The entire front here consists of such positions – always in visual distance of one another. The 50mm *PaK* and the mortar are also dug in as well as possible. One day is the same as the next.
>
> "Sun, sand and heat, and over everything circle a million flies. Only the daily fire from the British artillery brings any variety. It is also depressing that our artillery can only rarely reply to this greeting due to a shortage of ammunition."

After a few weeks in a foxhole, Hans Hesse was detailed to the Division Command post of the 164th Light Africa Division at Sidi Abd El Rachman and became the personal clerk of the Division Commander *Generalmajor [U.S. Brigadier General]* Langerhausen. He describes his first meeting with *General* Langerhausen this way:

> "His appearance amused me. He wore an English shirt with no shoulderboards, English trousers, shoes and socks – nothing of his outward appearance gave any indication that he was a *General.*"

Nachfolgend einige Auszüge aus dem Tagebuch des Obergefreiten Hans Hesse, der Mitte Juli 1942 zum Panzer Grenadier Rgt 433 (164. leichte Afrika Division) nach Nordafrika kam:

"Kampfraum El Alamein: Mit Spitzhacke und Schaufel hat sich unser Zug eine Igel-Stellung (Rundumverteidigungsstellung) aus dem steinigen Boden ausgehoben. Die ganze Front besteht hier aus solchen Igeln – immer in Sichtweitenentfernung. So gut es ging wurde auch die 5 cm PaK und der Granatwerfer eingegraben. Die Tage vergehen einer wie der andere.

Sonne, Sand, Hitze und über allem kreisen Millionen Fliegen. Abwechslung bringt nur der tägliche Beschuss durch die britische Artillerie. Deprimierend ist auch, das unsere Artillerie diese Grüsse wegen Munitionsmangel nur selten erwiedern kann".

Nach einigen Wochen im Deckungsloch wurde Hans Hesse zum Divisions-Gefechtsstand der 164. leichten Afrika Division bei Sidi Abd El Rachman abkommandiert und persönlicher Schreiber vom damaligen Divisions-Kommandeur Generalmajor Lungershausen. Seine erste Begegnung mit General Lungershausen beschreibt er so:

"Sein Auftreten amüsierte mich. Er trug ein englisches Hemd ohne Schulterklappen, eine englische Hose, Schuhe und Strümpfe – nichts an seinem Äusseren liess den General erkennen".

Pages 117-120: Informed of the threatening situation after the British counterattack on the El Alamein front, Field Marshal Rommel broke off his rest leave at home and returned to Africa on October 25, 1942. With a concerned expression, he listens to his commander's reports.

Seiten 117-120: Von der bedrohlichen Lage nach dem britischen Gegenangriff an der Alamein Front informiert, bricht Feldmarschall Rommel sofort seinen Genesungsurlaub in der Heimat ab und kehrt am 25. Oktober 1942 nach Nordafrika zurück. Mit sorgenvollem Gesichtsausdruck hört er sich die Berichte seiner Kommandeure an.

Second from the left is a *Luftwaffe FlaK Major* with an Army field cap. The cap's Army national eagle emblem has been removed and replaced with the *Luftwaffe* version.

Als zweiter von links ist ein Major der LW-Flak mit einer Heeres-Feldmütze zu sehen. Bei dieser Mütze ist der Heeres-Hoheitsadler entfernt worden und durch einen LW-Hoheitsadler ersetzt worden.

A colonel of the *Panzer* troops has his back turned to the camera. He too, is wearing a new-looking uniform. In the right background of the picture is a cameraman, who is catching this scene on film.

Ein Oberst der Panzertruppe hat dem Fotografen den Rücken zugekehrt. Er trägt auch eine noch sehr neu aussehende Uniform. Im rechten Bildhintergrund ist ein Kameramann zu sehen, der diese Szene im Film festhält.

AFRIKAKORPS

A Knight's Cross winner and Colonel of Reconnaissance troops briefs Rommel on the current situation using a map. He is wearing an enlisted man's tunic with its machine-woven national emblem and collar tabs. His cap is also an enlisted man's, thus without the officer's silver piping.* To the right behind Rommel, stands a *Luftwaffe Flak* officer with a field cap that was surely tailor made. [**Usually made of aluminum woven mesh cord – Transl.*]

Ein Oberst und Ritterkreuzträger der Aufklärungstruppen erläutert Rommel an Hand einer Karte die aktuelle Lage. Er trägt eine Mannschafts-Feldbluse mit deren gewebtem Hoheitsadler und Kragenspiegeln. Auch seine Feldmütze ist die der Mannschaftsdienstgrade, also ohne offiziersmässiger Silberpaspelierung. Rechts hinter Rommel steht ein Oberst der LW-Flak mit einer wohl vom Schneider stammenden Feldmütze.

Field Marshal Rommel is wearing a new tropical uniform with visor cap and high leather boots. *Hauptmann* [*Captain*] Berndt (left), originally detailed to Africa as the representative of the *Reichs* Press Chief, functions as Rommel's orderly. Right after this, Rommel sent Captain Berndt to report to the *Führer* headquarters, in order for him to request from Hitler a free hand in leading the *Afrikakorps*. While the majority of the officers seen here wear the comfortable long trousers, Berndt still wears breeches and with them the high tropical lace-up boots. An officer's leather belt and pistol holster is hanging on the folding stool in the foreground.

Feldmarschall Rommel trägt eine neue Tropenuniform mit Schirmmütze und hohe lederne Schaftstiefel. Hauptmann Berndt (links), urspünglich als Vertreter des Reichs-Pressechefs nach Afrika kommandiert, fungierte als Ordonanzoffizier Rommels. Unmittelbar darauf entsandte Rommel Hauptmann Berndt zur Berichterstattung ins Führerhauptquartier, um sich von Hitler volle Handlungsfreiheit für die Führung des Afrikakorps zu erbitten. Während die meisten, der hier zu sehenden Offiziere, die bequemeren langen Hosen tragen, trägt Berndt noch Breeches-Hosen und dazu die hohen Tropen-Schnürstiefel. An einem Klappstuhl im Vordergrund hängt ein Offiziers-Lederkoppel mit Pistolentasche.

More from the diary of Hans Hesse:

"During the night of 23-24 October the Gates of Hell broke open. A thousand English guns fired on our positions. Then came their tanks. We had already destroyed 100, but the English reserves are just too great. The Italians have already left their positions and fled without weapons. On an hourly schedule, the "*Sturen* 16" (British bomber squadron) ["*pigheaded 16*"] now attack our rearward positions and unload their deadly cargo. Rommel comes every three days in his personal vehicle, escorted by an armoured reconnaissance vehicle and his "Mammoth" command car, for a conference in our command post. One time, as he wanted to leave again after the meeting, the first bombs had already begun falling. Rommel jumped into the nearest foxhole and landed on the back of a radioman on our staff. Without turning around, the man shouted at Rommel: "You stupid dog! Look where you're jumping!" As the radioman then turned around he was thoroughly horrified, but Rommel only patted him on the shoulder in comradely fashion.

"The British succeeded in their breakthrough and on the night of the 1st through the 2nd of November our command post also came under constant artillery fire. Our heavy artillery is also firing now – they finally got some ammunition, or else the reserves were freed for use. I am hunkering in a foxhole with a signals man. He brought his backpack radio with him and set it to a German station. The song "Lili Marlen" rings out and tears roll down his cheeks. At dawn the area around our command post near the white mosque has also become a battlefield. English Armor is advancing. Suddenly our tanks appear, a murderous duel breaks out and we are stuck in the middle. Rounds are flying everywhere. We prefer to stay in our foxhole and attract as little attention as possible. In a short while, the field is covered with burning tanks from both sides. It's a horrible image – hardly anyone can come out of that alive. The command to withdraw has finally come, and is shouted from foxhole to foxhole."

Only a few hours later Hans Hesse was badly wounded after being hit in the thigh by a shell splinter and was brought to a field hospital by his comrades.

Weiter aus dem Tagebuch von Hans Hesse:
"In der Nacht vom 23. zum 24. Oktober brachen die Pforten der Hölle auf. Tausende englische Geschütze feuerten auf unsere Stellungen. Danach kamen ihre Panzer. 100 haben wir schon abgeschossen, aber die Reserven der Engländer sind einfach zu gross. Die Italiener haben schon ihre Stellungen verlassen und flüchten ohne Waffen. Im Stundentakt greifen jetzt auch die "sturen 16" (Britische Bomberstaffel) unsere rückwärtigen Einheiten an und entladen ihre tödliche Fracht. Alle 3 Tage kommt Rommel mit seinem PKW, begleitet von einem Panzerspähwagen und seinem Mammut Befehlswagen zur Besprechung in unserem Gefechtsstand. Einmal, als er danach wieder losfahren wollte, fielen auch schon die ersten Bomben. Rommel spang in das nächste Deckungsloch und landete auf dem Rücken eines Funkers aus unserem Stab. Ohne sich umzudrehen schrie dieser Rommel an: "Blöder Hund, pass doch auf, wo du hinspringst". Als sich der Funker dann umschaute, erschrak er gewaltig, doch Rommel klopfte ihm nur kameradschaftlich auf die Schulter".

"Den Briten ist der Durchbruch gelungen und in der Nacht vom 1. zum 2. November lag auch unser Gefechtsstand unter dem Dauerbeschuss ihrer Artillerie. Unsere schwere Artillerie feuerte jetzt auch. Endlich haben sie Munitionsnachschub bekommen – oder die Reserve-munition wurde freigegeben. Ich hocke mit einem Nachrichtenmann im Deckungsloch. Er hatte sein Tornister-Funkgerät mitgenommen und einen deutschen Sender eingestellt. Das Lied "Lilli Marleen" erklingt und ihm laufen Tränen über die Backen. Im Morgengrauen wird auch das Gebiet um unseren Gefechtsstand bei der weissen Moschee zum Gefechtsfeld. Englische Panzer rücken vor. Da tauchen auch unsere Panzer auf, ein mörderisches Duell entbrennt und wir sitzen mittendrin. Die Luft ist extrem eisenhaltig. Wir ziehen es vor im Deckungsloch zu bleiben und möglichst nicht aufzufallen. In kurzer Zeit ist das Schlachtfeld mit brennenden Panzern beider Seiten übersät. Es ist ein grauenvolles Bild, da kommt kaum einer lebend raus. Endlich ist der Befehl zum Rückzug gekommen und wird von Deckungs-loch zu Deckungsloch weitergerufen".

Wenige Stunden später wurde Hans Hesse durch einen Granatsplitter am Oberschenkel schwer verletzt und von Kameraden in ein Feldlazarett gebracht.

• • •

Although Rommel had received the order to hold the El Alamein position from Hitler and Mussolini, he decided after a consultation with the *Luftwaffe* Supreme Commander South, Field Marshal Kesselring, to ignore this order and on 3 November 1942 commanded a complete withdrawal, in order to save the *Afrikakorps* from threatening destruction.

Obwohl Feldmarschall Rommel von Hitler und Mussolini den Befehl zum Halten der Alamein-Stellung erhalten hatte, entschloss sich Rommel, nach Rücksprache mit dem Luft-waffen-Oberbefehlshaber Süd Feldmarschall Kesselring, diesen Befehl zu ignorieren und befahl am 3. November 1942 den kompletten Rückzug, um das Afrikakorps vor der drohenden Vernichtung zu bewahren.

Rommel succeeded in disengaging the majority of his troops from the enemy and lead them back in an orderly withdrawal in the direction of Libya. The paratroop brigade Ramcke, located in the southern sector of the front, succeeded in a particularly dashing stroke. Most of its vehicles had been destroyed by earlier artillery fire, but *General* Ramcke did not think of giving up. The elements of his unit that he could do without were sent away in the direction of the Libyan border with the last available truck. In a forced march, carrying their weapons along with them, the remainder started on their way. The antitank guns and crews, which served as the rear guard, still destroyed a few of the advancing British tanks. During the night of 5 November, the paratroopers ran into a long British military column. They jumped up on the vehicles and threw off the completely surprised Brits. They were now motorized again, and made it through to their own lines once more on 7 November. [*The German paratroopers had come across an entire bivouaced British supply column (for an armor unit) during the night. They captured all the vehicles from the surprised British without firing a shot, along with precious food, water and fuel supplies. By the time the paratroopers reached German lines again, they had covered some two hundred miles. For this feat, Ramcke was awarded the Oakleaves to the Knights Cross. – Transl.*]

Rommel schaffte es, den grössten Teil seiner Truppen vom Gegner zu lösen und geordnet in Richtung Libyen zurückzuführen. Der im südlichen Frontabschnitt liegenden Fallschirmjägerbrigade Ramcke gelang ein besonderes Husarenstück. Durch den vorangegangenen Artillerie-beschuss war der grösste Teil ihrer Fahrzeuge zerstört worden. Aber Generalmajor Ramcke dachte nicht an Aufgabe. Entbehrliche Teile seiner Einheit wurden mit den letzten noch vorhandenen Lastwagen in Richtung libyscher Grenze weggeschickt. Im Fussmarsch, unter mitführung ihrer Waffen, machten sie sich auf den langen Weg. Die die Nachhut bildenden Panzerjäger vernichteten noch etliche der nachrückenden britischen Panzer. In der Nacht zum 5. November stiessen die Fallschirmjäger auf eine lange britische Militärkolonne. Sie sprangen auf die Wagen und warfen die völlig überraschten Briten runter. Nun waren sie wieder motorisiert und am 7. November stiessen sie dann wieder zu den eigenen Truppen.

Sections of a reconnaissance battalion on the withdrawal. At the same time, the cautiously advancing British were kept at a distance by fast, fully motorized rear guard units.

Teile einer Aufklärungsabteilung auf dem Rückzug. Die vorsichtig nachrückenden Briten wurden derweil von schnellen, voll motorisierten Nachhutverbänden auf Distanz gehalten.

WH

Endless columns travel rearward.

Endlose Kolonnen fahren zurück.

This heavy eighteen ton *Famo* towing vehicle had to be left behind due to motor damage. In order to prevent the British from being able to put it to further use under their colors, it is set on fire.

Diese schwere 18 to. Famo-Zugmaschine musste wegen eines Motorschadens aufgegeben werden. Damit die Briten nichts mehr damit anfangen können, ist sie in Brand gesetzt worden.

This Me 109 fighter's landing gear was damaged during an emergency landing. To prevent it from falling into the hands of the advancing British and being salvaged for use, it too, is set ablaze – the quickest way to accomplish this was by throwing a hand grenade into the cockpit.

Dieses Me 109 Jagdflugzeug hat bei einer Notlandung einen Fahrwerksbruch erlitten. Da es vor den nachrückenden Briten nicht rechtzeitig geborgen werden konnte, wurde es ebenfalls in Brand gesetzt – am schnellsten ging das, indem eine Handgranate ins Cockpit geworfen wurde.

In the Arab settlements, German soldiers were always warmly welcomed. In exchange for tea, sugar and other things, the Germans received fresh eggs.

In den Araber-Siedlungen wurden die Deutschen Soldaten wie immer freundlich begrüsst. Im Tausch gegen Tee, Zucker und sonstiges erhalten die Deutschen frische Hühnereier.

From November 7, 1942, strong American and British units had been landing in Algeria and Morocco, and after defeating the French colonial troops there, quickly moved on Tunisia. Even Hitler had realized meanwhile that the potential loss of all of North Africa loomed over them. After consultation with and approval of the French President Marshal Pétain (Vichy Government), the first German security units had been landed on 11 November in Tunisia. One by one, additional German units were transferred to Tunisia, so that a strong bridgehead could be built there. These units* threw back the Allied troops that had already advanced far into Tunisia. The German-Italian units meanwhile, had to gradually give up Libya. Cities like Tobruk, Dema and Benghazi, which had cost so much blood and deprivation during their recapture months earlier, had to be left to the British practically uncontested. Rommel, who already knew the hopelessness of the overall military situation, still hoped for a reasonable course from Hitler that would allow him to lead his troops from Tunisia back to Italy. [**Fallschirmjäger Regiment 5 (Paratroop Rgt.) under command of Oberstleutnant (Lieutenant Colonel) Koch, and the "Barenthin Regiment" under Oberst [Colonel] Walther Barenthin (formed from various Paratroop units) were sent in; these stopped the Allies at Mateur and Tebourba on 29 November. – Transl.]*

Seit dem 7. November 1942 waren in Algerien und Marokko starke amerikanisch/britische Verbände angelandet worden, die nach dem Niederkämpfen von Französischen Kolonialtruppen rasch auf Tunesien vorrückten. Inzwischen hatte auch Hitler eingesehen, dass der Verlust von ganz Nordafrika zu befürchten war. Nach Rücksprache und mit Genehmigung des französischen Staatspräsidenten Marschall Pétain (Vichy-Regierung) waren die ersten deutschen Sicherungsverbände am 11. November 1942 in Tunesien gelandet. Zug um Zug wurden weitere deutsche Einheiten nach Tunesien verlegt, um hier einen starken Brückenkopf zu bilden. Bereits weit nach Tunesien eingedrungene alliierte Truppen wurden von ihnen erfolgreich zurückgeworfen. Derweil mussten die deutsch-italienischen Verbände wieder schrittweise Libyen aufgeben. Städte wie Tobruk, Derna, und Bengasi, deren Rückeroberung vor Monaten viel Blut und Entbehrungen gekostet hatte, mussten nun nahezu kampflos den Briten überlassen werden. Rommel, dem die Aussichtslosigkeit der gesamten militärischen Lage bereits bewusst war, hoffte immer noch auf ein Einlenken Hitlers, damit er von Tunesien aus seine Truppen nach Italien zurückführen konnte.

Photos taken most likely in the area of the Libyan-Tunisian border.

Fotos die wahrscheinlich im libysch/tunesischen Grenzgebiet aufgenommen worden sind.

In his open commander's vehicle, Field Marshal Rommel meets with Italian troops in the area of the Mareth-Line of the Tunisian – Libyan border defenses. To his left, the Italian Chief of the General Staff Marshal Count Cavallero is visible, and with his back to the camera stands the German Chief of Staff, Colonel Bayerlein.

Feldmarschall Rommel ist mit seinem offenen Kommandeurswagen bei italienischen Truppen im Bereich der Mareth-Linie, der tunesisch – libyschen Grenzbefestigungen, eingetroffen. Links neben ihm ist der italienische Generalstabschef Marschall Graf Cavallero zu sehen. Mit dem Rücken zum Fotografen steht der deutsche Stabschef Oberst Bayerlein.

Marshal Count Cavallero and Field Marshal Rommel.

Marschall Graf Cavallero und Feldmarschall Rommel.

Field Marshal Rommel.

Feldmarschall Rommel.

Rommel with Italian officers. He is wearing a long coat with the *Afrikakorps* cufftitle. In his hand he's holding the so-called "intermediate baton" – this is the field staff, which was used in the field in place of his Marshal's baton.* This picture and the three previous as well, were probaly taken around the beginning of February 1943. At the beginning of March 1943, Rommel was recalled from Tunisia in order to restore his weakened health. [**See Glossary under "Marshal's Staff" – Transl.*]

Rommel mit italienischen Offizieren. Er trägt einen langen Mantel mit dem Afrikakorps Ärmelband. In der Hand hält er den sogenannten Interimsstab. Das ist der feldmässige Ersatz für seinen Marschallsstab. Dieses und die 3 vorigen Fotos stammen vermutlich von Anfang Februar 1943. Anfang März 1943 wurde Rommel aus Tunesien abberufen um seine angegriffene Gesundheit wiederherstellen zu lassen.

The new commander of the 164th Light Africa Division, Brigadier *General* Baron von Liebenstein (seated in the *Kübelwagen*), listens to a Lieutenant's report. *Generals* normally wore visor caps with gold piping and gilt metal insignia (silver insignia was used prior to 1942, though piping and chin cords were gold) – von Liebenstein, however, wears a [*non-general grade*] officer's visor cap instead, with silver insignia and the pink piping of Armor troops.* Only the gold chin cords indicate his *General*'s rank. Due to the shortage of tropical rank insignia, his driver, a *Panzer* Grenadier corporal, wears shoulderboards and corporal's rank chevrons from the continental *Wehrmacht* uniform. On the door and below the black-white-red Divison Commander's pennant, is the divisional insignia of the 64th Light Africa Division – crossed "Meissen" swords over the African continent. The Meissen swords are the logo of the renowned porcelain that originated from Meissen near Dresden, and these became a part of the divisional insignia since most of the regiments that belonged to the 164th Light Africa Division came from the area around Dresden. (**See the glossary under "Uniforms."*)

Der neue Kommandeur der 164. leichten Afrika-Division Generalmajor Freiherr von Liebenstein (im Kübelwagen sitzend) hört sich den Bericht eines Leutnants an. Regulär tragen Generäle Schirmmützen mit goldener Paspelierung, und goldenen Effekten – von Liebenstein trägt hier jedoch eine offiziersmässige Schirmmütze mit silbernen Effekten und der rosa Paspelierung der Panzertruppe. Lediglich die goldene Mützenkordel weisst auf seinen Generalsrang hin. Sein Fahrer, ein Obergefreiter der Panzer Grenadiere trägt in Ermangelung von Rangabzeichen in der Tropen-Version, Schulterklappen und Obergefreiten-winkel der kontinentalen Wehrmachtsuniform. Auf der Tür und unter dem schwarz-weiss-roten Divisions-Kommandeursstanders des Kübelwagens ist das Divisionsabzeichen der 164. leichten Afrika-Division zu sehen – gekreuzte Meissen-Schwerter über dem afrikanischen Kontinent. Die Meissen-Schwerter sind das Markenzeichen des berühmten Porzellans aus Meissen bei Dresden und wurden Bestandteil des Divisionsabzeichens, weil die meisten der zur 164. lei. Afrika Div. gehörenden Regimenter aus der Umgebung von Dresden kamen.

General von Liebenstein viewing positions. On his right breast pocket he wears a hand-embroidered cloth version of the German Cross in Gold award. [*The cloth version was hand-embroidered on a felt backing. It was preferred by some officers due to the weight of the metal version. – Transl.*]

General von Liebenstein (rechts) bei der Besichtigung von Stellungen. Auf seiner rechten Brusttasche trägt er eine gestickte Stoffvariante des Deutschen Kreuz in Gold.

General von Liebenstein in a village in the vicinity of the Mareth Line.

General von Liebenstein in einem Dorf in der Nähe der Mareth Linie.

A 105mm Howitzer firing. Several white rings are painted on the gun tube; each ring stands for the direct fire destruction of an enemy armored vehicle.

Eine 10,5 cm Feldhaubitze beim Abschuss. Auf dem Geschütz-Rohr sind mehrere weisse Ringe aufgemalt. Jeder Ring steht für einen direkten Abschuss eines gepanzerten gegnerischen Fahrzeugs.

Two 210mm long-bore guns in a firefight.

Zwei 21 cm Langrohrgeschütze im Feuergefecht.

A captured British light personnel carrier (type Bren?) is inspected. Photographs from the Tunisian combat area above all, prove that captured Allied equipment was employed on a large scale by the German side.

Ein erbeuteter leichter britischer Schützenpanzer (Typ Bren Carrier ?) wird untersucht. Vor allem vom tunesischen Kampfraum ist durch Fotos belegt, dass erbeutetes alliiertes Kriegsgerät in grossem Umfang auf deutscher Seite eingesetzt wurde.

Opposite: The Chief of Staff Fritz Bayerlein, promoted to Brigadier *General* in March 1943, in a conversation with *Sonderführer* [*technical specialist*] Moosmüller (propaganda company). Standing between them in the background is Rommel's interpreter, *Sonderführer* Dr. Franz. Some interesting details for uniform study are also visible in this photograph. The artillery Lieutenant (left) is wearing a pair of *Luftwaffe* pouch pocket trousers along with his field tunic, which has standard officer accouterments. The soutache chevron has been removed from his cap. One can only see the light shadow where it was once attached. *General* Bayerlein is wearing a cufftitle, which I would identify as the "*Afrika*" campaign cufftitle (with palms) – except that this would place it sewn on the wrong sleeve [*this campaign cufftitle was introduced in January 1943 – Transl.*]. His German Cross* as well, which, according to regulations, should be worn at the center of the right breast pocket, he has pinned on in sloppy fashion. He did not particularly care for this award due to the large swastika on it.** Around the buttonhole on his left breast pocket one can see a blue ribbon with a small star mounted on it; this is the method of wear in the field for a high Italian award. Interpreter Doctor Franz (third from the left) likewise wears this Italian award. He also wears the 1939 Spange* to the Iron Cross 2nd Class on the World War I pattern black and white ribbon*, and the silver *Panzer* Assault Badge.* Moosmüller is not wearing any collar tabs on his tunic. The darker areas on the collar indicate that the tabs were there, but have been removed. [**See Glossary under "Awards"; **See P. Spayd's biography "Bayerlein: From Afrikakorps to Panzer Lehr", Schiffer Publishing Ltd. 2003, for more on the negative views toward National Socialism held by Rommel's Chief of Staff and close associate – Transl.*]

Gegenüberliegende Seite: Der im März 1943 zum Generalmajor beförderte Stabschef Fritz Bayerlein im Gespräch mit Sonderführer Moosmüller (Propagandakompanie). Zwischen ihnen im Hintergrund steht Rommel's Dolmetscher, Sonderführer Dr. Franz. Auch auf diesem Foto sind wieder einige interessante uniformkundliche Details zu sehen. Der Artillerie-Leutnant (links) trägt zur Heeres-Feldbluse mit Standard Offiziers-Effekten eine Luftwaffenhose mit Beintasche. An seiner Feldmütze ist der Soutachewinkel entfernt worden. Man sieht nur noch den leichten Schatten, wo er einmal war. General Bayerlein trägt ein Ärmelband, welches ich wegen des kurzen Schriftzuges als das "Afrika"-Ärmelband (mit Palmen) identifizieren würde – allerdings wäre es dann am falschen Ärmel angenäht worden. Auch sein Deutsches Kreuz, welches laut Vorschrift auf der Mitte der rechten Brusttasche zu tragen war, hat er sehr salopp angesteckt. Wegen des grossen Hakenkreuzes darauf, mochte er diesen Orden auch nicht sonderlich leiden. Um das Knopfloch seiner linken Brusttasche sieht man ein blaues Ordensband mit einem darauf sitzenden kleinen Stern befestigt. Dies ist die feldmässige Trageweise einer hohen italienischen Auszeichnung. Dolmetscher Dr. Franz (3. von links) trägt ebenfalls diese italienische Auszeichnung. Desweitern trägt er die Wiederholungsspange zum Eisernen Kreuz 2. Klasse auf dem schwarz-weissen Ordensband und das silberne Panzer-Kampfabzeichen. Moosmüller trägt an seiner Feldbluse gar keine Kragenspiegel. An den dunkleren Stellen des Kragens ist zu sehen, dass die Kragenspiegel entfernt wurden.

From left to right: Moosmüller, Dr. Franz, and Bayerlein.

Von Links nach rechts: Moosmüller, Dr. Franz, Bayerlein.

Right: Brigadier *General* Schnarrenberger and a Colonel greet one another.

Rechts: Generalmajor Schnarrenberger und ein Oberst begrüssen sich.

Once again out on a scouting mission with the VW "tub."

Wieder geht es mit dem VW-Kübel auf Erkundungsfahrt.

The mountainous interior of Tunisia has to be reconnoitered.

Das bergige Landesinnere Tunesiens soll erkundet werden.

A village schoolteacher with his sons hikes with the German soldiers up a mountain, from where they will have a good view of the surrounding area.

Ein Dorfschullehrer und seine Söhne steigen mit den Deutschen Soldaten auf einen Berg, von dem sie eine gute Aussicht auf die Umgebung haben.

In a mountain village they meet up with comrades who have arrived there in a truck. Curious villagers gather around the foreigners.

In einem Bergdorf treffen sie auf Kameraden, die mit einem LKW hierher gekommen sind. Neugierig umlagern die Dorfbewohner die Fremden.

The children also marvel at the foreigners and their vehicles.

Auch die Kinder der Dorfbewohner bestaunen die Fremden und ihre Fahrzeuge.

These comrades have set up their tents in a small hollow in a valley. After the rigors of the long withdrawal through the Libyan desert they can relax a little here, protected from direct enemy observation. Some enjoy the warm rays of the spring sun, while others use the time to write another field mail letter home to the family.

Diese Kameraden haben ihre Zelte in einem kleinen Talkessel aufgeschlagen. Nach den Strapazen des langen Rückzugs durch die libysche Wüste können sie sich hier, geschützt vor direkter Feindeinsicht, ein wenig ausruhen. Einige geniessen die wärmenden Strahlen der Frühlingssonne, andere nutzen die Zeit um mal wieder einen Feldpostbrief an die Familie zu schreiben.

The mountainous interior of Tunisia and the more luxurient vegetation offer better possibilities for cover than the Libyan/Egyptian desert. Here a tent is set up, well camouflaged between the trees.

Das gebirgige Landesinnere Tunesiens und die üppigere Vegetation bieten wesentlich bessere Deckungsmöglichkeiten als die libysch-ägyptische Wüste. Hier wurde gut getarnt zwischen den Bäumen ein Zelt aufgeschlagen.

At the edge of a field protected by cactuses, surrounded by blossoming almond and olive trees, the men from the propaganda company have set up their tents.

Am Rande eines durch eine Kakteenhecke geschützten Feldes, umgeben von blühenden Mandel- und Olivenbäumen, haben die Männer von der Propagandakompanie ihre Zelte aufgeschlagen.

For protection against air attacks, this tent is partially dug into the earth. The dual-layered tent roof construction can also be quite clearly recognized here. The air space between the two sheets acts as an insolation layer, to keep the heat of the day out of the tent interior. Since the German soldiers in Tunisia had ample supplies of water available, uniforms and underwear could be given a real wash here. The laundry is hung up to dry on a clothesline run between the tents. The field cap, washed along with the laundry, hangs on a stick.

Zum Schutz vor Luftangriffen ist dieses Zelt teilweise in den Boden eingegraben worden. Hier ist auch gut der zweischichtige Aufbau des Zeltdachs zu erkennen. Der Luftspalt zwischen den Planen wirkt als Isolierschicht, um die Tageshitze vom Zeltinneren abzuhalten. Da den deutschen Soldaten in Tunesien wieder ausreichend Wasser zur Verfügung stand, konnten hier auch mal wieder die Uniformen und die Unterwäsche richtig gewaschen werden. Die Wäsche ist zum Trocknen auf die Abspannleinen des Zeltes zum Trocknen aufgehangen worden. Die ebenfalls mitgewaschene Feldmütze hängt auf einem Stock.

It is now about time to introduce the man who took most of these pictures. Eberhard Dohm, a photographer in the propaganda company – marked by the deprivations of the desert. Here in a shirt, tropical shorts, an Army enlisted man's webbed canvas belt with a pistol holster, and a faded field cap.

Jetzt wird es auch mal Zeit, den Mann vorzustellen, von dem die meisten dieser Fotos stammen. Eberhard Dohm, Fotograf in der Propagandakompanie – von den Entbehrungen der Wüste gezeichnet. Hier im Hemd, kurzer Tropenhose, Heeres-Mannschafts-Webkoppel mit aufgeschlaufter Pistolentasche und ausgeblichener Feldmütze.

As one doesn't want to be seen in public with such a shabby appearance, a canister of water is brought from the nearest well.

Da man sich aber so runtergekommen nicht gern der Öffentlichkeit zeigt, wird vom nächsten Brunnen erst einmal ein Kanister Wasser geholt.

Eberhard Dohm "bathing", with upper body completely lathered. A bucket serves as a washbasin, which sits atop the water canister. The canister, painted a sand color, bears in addition to the painted white cross, the stamped nomenclature "Water 20 l" (liter), "1942" as the year of manufacture, the manufacturer's company mark, and "*Wehrmacht*".

Eberhard Dohm, mit komplett eingeseiftem Oberkörper beim "Baden". Als Waschtisch dient eine Schüssel, die auf dem Wasserkanister steht. Der sandfarbig lackierte Wasserkanister trägt neben dem auflackiertem weissen Kreuz, die eingeprägten Bezeichnungen: "Wasser 20 l" (Liter), "1942" als Herstellungsjahr, das Hersteller-Firmenzeichen und "Wehrmacht".

Freshly washed, beard shaved as well as possible, a totally different looking Eberhard Dohm presents himself. On the left side breast pocket of his tunic he has put on a Sports badge, and in the highest buttonhole he has affixed the ribbon for the War Merit Cross 2nd Class.* Beneath the field tunic he wears a "V" neck pullover sweater and a scarf. On his chest hangs his private purchase Leica camera, with which he took most of these photos. [**See the Glossary under "Awards".*]

Frisch gewaschen, den Bart so gut es ging abgeschabt, präsentiert sich jetzt ein ganz anders aussehender Eberhard Dohm. Auf der linken Brusttasche der Feldbluse hat er ein Sportabzeichen angesteckt und im obersten Knopfloch das Ordensband des Kriegs-Verdienstkreuz 2. Klasse befestigt. Unter der Feldbluse trägt er einen Pullover mit V-förmigen Halsausschnitt und ein Halstuch. Vor der Brust hängt sein privater Leica-Fotoapparat, mit der er die meisten dieser Fotos aufgenommen hat.

Shortly before the surrender of the German-Italian troops on the 12th and 13th of May in Tunisia, Eberhard Dohm was able to leave North Africa. The following section shows pictures that he took during the subsequent fighting on the island of Sicily.

Kurz vor der Kapitulation der deutsch-italienischen Truppen am 12./13. Mai 1943 in Tunesien konnte Eberhard Dohm noch Nordafrika verlassen. Das nachfolgende Kapitel zeigt Aufnahmen, die er während der nachfolgenden Kämpfe auf der Insel Sizilien aufgenommen hat.

• • •

Sicily

During combat operations in North Africa, the Italian Mediterranean island of Sicily was an important factor for the Italian and German Army as a staging point for re-supply convoys and as a base for *Luftwaffe* units.

After the capitulation of the German-Italian *Afrikakorps* on the 12th and 13th May 1943, the remainder of various German units were still on the island. The *Wehrmacht* leadership was aware that it was sure to be the next Allied target, and so the remnants here of the *Luftwaffe* "*Hermann Göring*" Division were re-manned and at the same time expanded into a Paratroop-*Panzer* Division. In addition the 15th *Panzer*-Grenadier Division and the XIVth *Panzer* Corps came under operational combined command of General Hube. Unter Italian command stood the Italian 6th Army, consisting of the 4th Infantry Division and the 5th Coastal Security Division.

After preparatory air attacks on the island lasting several weeks, the Allied landing operation "Husky" began on 10 July 1941. With a huge number of warships and transport vessels, they shipped the American 7th Army under General Patton and the British 8th Army under Montgomery there from North Africa. Under the protection of 3500 combat aircraft and the heavy ship artillery they succeeded in landing on the Sicilian coast relatively unhindered, all the more so as the Italian-German side had no definitive knowledge of the Allied targets and no landing was expected due to the stormy seas at that time. And so the defense of the island only really got underway in the next days following the landing, in which the Germans once again had to carry the brunt of the fighting. In the face of the Allied materiel superiority the Italian troops in many cases, had already deserted after a few days.

On the 25th of July 1943 the Italian dictator Mussilini was removed from power and put under arrest by his followers. In view of the hopelessness of the military situation and the unstable political situation, the island was evacuated step by step, with hardly any notice by the Allies. On August 17, 1943 the last of the defenders left the island along with most of their equipment

Eberhard Dohm, the war reporter now familiar to us, was ordered back to Italy from Tunisia in April of 1943, before the capitulation of the Axis troops. He saw further action after this in Sicily and Sourthern Italy. The following photos remain from that time period. At a date that can't be exactly determined, he was taken prisoner in Southern Italy by Allied forces. After his release from imprisonment, he returned to his hometown of Bielefeld, where he worked as a photographer. He died there in 1956, at the age of fifty-seven.

Sizilien

Während der Kampfhandlungen in Nord-Afrika war die italienische Mittelmeerinsel Sizilien ein wichtiger Faktor für die italienische und deutsche Armee, als Ausgangspunkt für Nachschub-Geleitzüge und als Stützpunkt von Luftwaffenverbänden.

Nach der Kapitulation des Deutsch-Italienischen Afrikakorps am 12./13. Mai 1943 waren noch Reste verschiedener Deutscher Einheiten auf der Insel. Der Wehrmachtsführung war bewusst, dass die Insel wohl das nächste Ziel der Alliierten sein würde. So wurde der hier verbliebene Rest der Luftwaffen Division "Hermann Göring" personalmässig wieder aufgefüllt unter gleichzeitiger Erweiterung zur Fallschirm-Panzerdivision. Desweiteren kam hier unter dem Gesamtkommando von General Hube die 15. Pz.-Grenadierdivision und das XIV. Panzer-Korps zum Einsatz. Unter italienischem Kommando stand die 6. italienische Armee, bestehend aus der 4. Infanteriedivision und der 5. Küstenschutzdivision.

Nach wochenlangen vorbereitenden Luftangriffen auf die Insel lief am 10. Juli 1943 die alliierte Landungsoperation "Husky"an. Mit einer gewaltigen Anzahl von Kriegs- und Transportschiffen setzten die amerikanische 7. Armee unter General Patton und die britische 8. Armee und General Montgomery von Nord-Afrika aus über. Unter dem Schutz von über 3500 Kampfflugzeugen und der schweren Schiffsartillerie gelang ihnen relativ ungehindert die Landung an der sizilianischen Küste. Zumal von italienisch – deutscher Seite keine gesicherten Erkenntnisse über die alliierten Angriffsziele vorlagen und wegen der stürmischen See für diesen Zeitpunkt keine Landung erwartet wurde. So lief die Verteidigung der Insel erst in den nächsten Tagen richtig an, wobei die Deutschen mal wieder die Hauptlast des Kampfes zu tragen hatten. Die italienischen Truppen liefen vielfach angesichts der allierten Übermacht bereits nach wenigen Tagen davon.

Am 25. Juli 1943 wurde der italienische Diktator Benito Mussolini von seinen eigenen Gefolgsleuten entmachtet und verhaftet. Angesichts der Aussichtslosigkeit der militärischen Lage und der instabilen politischen Lage wurde die Insel, von den Allierten weitgehend unbemerkt, schrittweise wieder geräumt. Am 17. August 1943 verliessen die letzten Verteidiger Siziliens unter Mitnahme des meisten Wehrgeräts die Insel.

Der uns bereits bekannte Kriegsberichterstatter Eberhard Dohm wurde im April 1943, vor der Kapitulation der Achsentruppen, aus Tunesien nach Italien zurückbeordert. Danach sah er weiteren Einsatz auf Sizilien und in Süd-Italien. Aus dieser Zeit sind die nachfolgenden Fotos erhalten geblieben. Zu einem nicht näher bekannten Zeitpunkt geriet er in Süd-Italien in alliierte Kriegsgefangenschaft. Nach der Rückkehr aus der Gefangenschaft arbeitete er als Fotograf in seiner Heimatstadt Bielefeld. Hier verstarb er 1965 im Alter von 57 Jahren.

The *Kübelwagen*'s ID, "WH 1275810" indicates that this vehicle entered the *Wehrmacht* inventory around May of 1942. Painted beside the ID mark is a stylized sailboat. This is the ID mark for a quartermaster battalion (re-supply and maintenance unit).

Das Kennzeichen des VW-Kübelwagens WH 1275810 zeigt an, dass dieses Fahrzeug etwa im Mai 1942 in den Fahrzeugbestand der Wehrmacht aufgenommen wurde. Neben dem Fahrzeug-Kennzeichen ist ein stilisiertes Segelboot aufgemalt worden. Es ist das Erkennungszeichen eines Feldzeug Bat. (Nachschub und Versorgungs-Einheit).

A VW *Kübelwagen* drives onto a ferry (a so-called "Siebel Ferry") to be transported over the few kilometers from the Italian mainland over the Straights of Messina to Sicily. Soldiers lay planks from the dock to the ferry, so that the vehicle can drive onto the loading surface. They can work here in relative security from Allied Aircraft, since both sides of the Straights of Messina are secured my strong *FlaK* units. With such "Siebel" ferries of the German Navy, even the heavy Tiger tanks were carried from Italy to Sicily and farther, over the open sea to Tunisia.

Ein VW-Kübelwagen fährt auf ein Fährschiff (sogenannte Siebelfähre), um vom italienischen Festland über die nur wenige Kilometer breite Meerenge von Messina auf die Insel Sizilien überzusetzen. Soldaten legen Planken vom Anlegesteg an die Fähre, damit der Wagen auf die Ladefläche fahren kann. Sie können hier relativ sicher vor alliierten Flugzeugen arbeiten, denn die Meerenge von Messina ist auf beiden Ufern von starken Flakeinheiten gesichert. Mit solchen Siebelfähren der Deutschen Kriegsmarine wurden sogar die schweren Tiger-Panzer von Italien nach Sizilien und weiter über das offene Meer nach Tunesien geschafft.

Eberhard Dohm has boarded a smaller ferry, in order to transfer to Sicily as well. The coxswain in his covered wheelhouse has turned the ferry and set course for the opposite bank. At the front right of the picture is the ferry's only armament – an MG34.[*] To its left, next to the passenger luggage is a pile of life jackets. [*MG = Maschinen-Gewehr = Machinegun; see Glossary under "Weapons" – Transl.]

Eberhard Dohm ist an Bord eines kleineren Fährschiffs gegangen, um ebenfalls nach Sizilien überzusetzen. Der Steuermann in seinem überdachten Ruderstand hat die Fähre gewendet und nimmt Kurs auf das gegenüberliegende Ufer. Vorn rechts im Bild ist die einzige Bewaffnung der Fähre zu sehen – ein MG 34. Links davon, neben dem Gepäck der Passagiere, liegt ein Stapel Schwimmwesten.

With a calm sea, the passengers enjoy the crossing. The sergeant (right) is an "Old Boy African" since he still wears an early model of the high* Army tropical lace-up boots and with them a pair of breeches. He has attached his decorations – the Infantry Assault Badge in Silver and the ribbon clasp of the Italo-German Campaign Medal – to his shirt. [**Tropical boots were issued in a knee-high model, and also in an ankle-high model that looked more like shoes – Transl.*]

Bei ruhiger See geniessen die Passagiere die Überfahrt. Der Feldwebel (rechts) ist ein "Alter Afrikaner", denn er trägt noch ein frühes Modell der hohen Heeres Tropen-Schnürstiefel und dazu Breecheshosen. Seine Auszeichnungen – das silberne Infanterie-Sturmabzeichen und die Bandspange der italienisch-deutschen Afrika-Feldzugsmedaille hat er sich an sein Hemd gesteckt.

It appears this soldier does not entirely trust the peaceful, idyllic scenery. He has cautiously donned a life vest. He too, seems to be an "Old Boy African", since his cap and trousers are heavily faded by the sun. Like most of his comrades he also wears the tropical ankle shoes, which were much more comfortable to wear and much quicker to put on than the high lace-up boots.

Dieser Soldat scheint der friedlichen Idylle nicht so ganz zu trauen, er hat vorsichtshalber eine Schwimmweste angelegt. Auch er scheint ein "Alter Afrikaner" zu sein, denn seine Mütze und Hose sind schon sehr stark von der Sonne ausgeblichen. Er trägt auch wie die meisten seinerKameraden die halbhohen Tropenschuhe, welche wesentlich angenehmer zu tragen und schneller anzuziehen waren als die hohen Schnürstiefel.

Thick smoke and ruins show that this Sicilian harbor has just been attacked by Allied bombers, in order to destroy the opposing infrastructure prior to the planned invasion.

Dichter Rauch und Trümmer zeigen, dass dieser sizilianische Hafen erst vor Kurzem von alliierten Bombern angegriffen worden ist, um die gegnerische Infrastruktur vor der geplanten Invasion zu zerstören.

This ship also fell victim to a bombing attack.

Auch dieses Schiff fiel den Bombenangriffen zum Opfer.

On an observation platform high above a small harbor, our photographer meets this soldier from a signal's unit. As a walking out uniform he still wears the complete early version of the tropical uniform with field tunic, shirt and tie, web belt and bayonett, breeches, high lace-up boots and a field cap with the yelllow soutache chevron of the Signals Troops.

Auf einer Aussichtsterasse, hoch über einem kleinen Hafen trifft unser Fotograf diesen Soldat einer Nachrichteneinheit. Als Ausgehuniform trägt er noch die komplette frühe Version der Tropen-Uniform mit Feldbluse, Hemd mit Binder, Webkoppel mit Bajonett, Breecheshose, hohen Schnürstiefeln und eine Feldmütze mit dem gelben Soutachewinkel der Nachrichtentruppe.

These *Luftwaffe* soldiers have a pass, as well. On a stone wall, sitting before a dreamlike coastal landscape, they gaze out over the expanse of the Mediterranean.

Auch diese Luftwaffensoldaten haben Ausgang. Auf einer Mauer, vor einer traumhaften Küstenlandschaft sitzend, blicken sie auf die Weite des Mittelmeeres.

A *Pionier* [Engineer] has a high polish returned to his tropical lace-up boots (1st model) by a roadside shoe shiner. In accordance with regulations, while out on pass, he wears his bayonet on the belt. He may also be an "Old Boy African", as his faded field cap with black soutache chevron seems to suggest.

Ein Pionier lässt sich seine Tropen-Schnürstiefel (1. Modell) von einem Strassen-Schuhputzer wieder auf Hochglanz bringen. Vorschriftsgemäss trägt der Pionier beim Ausgang sein Bajonett am Koppel. Er könnte auch ein "Alter Afrikaner" sein, wie seine ausgeblichene Feldmütze mit schwarzem Soutachewinkel vermuten lässt.

Far removed from the horrors of war, these soldiers have made themselves comfortable. They have carried stools and chairs from their quarters outside, and enjoy the warming rays of the spring sun with a bottle of Sekt. The Master Sergeant (left) wears the field gray version of the *Panzer* uniform, as worn by assault gun units and from March 1943, also by the crews of self-propelled guns of the *Panzer-Grenadiere*.* Two parallel horizontal rings are sewn on his sleeve. These so-called "Piston rings" were the mark of recognition for the company First Sergeant – also called a "*Spiess*". [**Panzer-Grenadiers = Armored Infantry – today usually referred to as "Mech" (mechanized) Infantry – Transl.*]

Weitab von den Schrecken des Krieges haben es sich diese Soldaten gemütlich gemacht. Sie haben Stühle und Sessel aus ihrer Unterkunft nach draussen getragen und geniessen bei einer Flasche Sekt die wärmenden Strahlen der Frühlingssonne. Der Ober-Feldwebel (links) trägt die feldgraue Version der Panzeruniform, wie sie von den Sturmgeschützeinheiten und ab März 1943 auch von den Besatzungen der Selbstfahrlafetten der Panzergrenadiere getragen wurde. Am Ärmel sind 2 umlaufende Litzen aufgenäht. Diese sogenannten "Kolbenringe" waren das Erkennungszeichen für einen Kompanie-Feldwebel – auch "Spiess" genannt.

Two *Panzer Grenadiers* on a terrain inspection. Both wear the field gray standard uniform worn by [*Army*] troops since 1940. As can be seen by the ribbons worn through the buttonholes, both soldiers have already been awarded the Iron Cross 2nd Class. The sergeant standing in the background has gotten to know the Russian winter, since he is also wearing the ribbon belonging to the medal "Winter Fighting in the East 1941-1942"* [*or, "Ostmedaille"- Transl.*] – referred to by most infantrymen with little respect as the "Frozen Meat Order." Interestingly enough, they are wearing the tropical webbed belt with their field gray uniform. Their field caps are the new Model 1943 (M43). This cap was developed from the similar *Bergmütze.*** (**See the Glossary under "Awards"; ** mountain cap – Transl.*]

2 Panzergrenadiere bei einer Geländebesichtigung. Beide tragen die feldgraue Standard-Uniform, wie sie seit 1940 bei der Truppe getragen wurde. Wie an den durch die Knopflöcher geschlauften Ordensbändern zu erkennen ist, wurde beiden Soldaten bereits das Eiserne Kreuz 2. Klasse verliehen. Der im Hintergrund stehende Feldwebel hat bereits den russischen Winter kennengelernt, denn er trägt auch noch das Ordensband der Medaille "Winterschlacht im Osten 1941-1942" – von den Landsern meist ziemlich respektlos "Gefrierfleisch-Orden" genannt. Interessanterweise tragen sie zur feldgrauen Uniform die Webstoff-Koppel der Tropenuniform. Ihre Feldmützen sind die des neuen Modells 1943 (M43). Diese Mützen sind aus den ähnlichen Bergmützen der Gebirgsjäger weiterentwickelt worden.

The climb into the still snow covered summit region of Aetna is arduous. The Mountain Troops give themselves and their heavily loaded pack animals a breather.

Der Aufstieg in die noch schneebedeckte Gipfelregion des Ätna ist mühselig. Die Gebirgsjäger gönnen sich und ihren schwer bepackten Lasttieren eine Verschnaufpause.

Mountain troops with their pack animals on a climb into the mountaintop region of Sicily's commanding volcanic massif of Aetna. The soldier at the center of the picture is wearing the windbreaker and mountain shoes typical for a Mountain Trooper.

Gebirgsjäger mit ihren Lasttieren beim Aufstieg in die Gipfelregion des die Insel Sizilien beherrschenden Vulkanmassivs des Ätna. Der Soldat in der Bildmitte trägt die für die Gebirgsjäger typische Windjacke und Bergschuhe.

The threatening invasion of Sicily still does not seem immediately apparent, and so freetime is used to reconnoiter the scenic beauty of the island by *Kübelwagen*. This "Tourist Group" presents itself here in front of an old fort. A camouflage net, completely interwoven with tufts of grass, is secured to the VW-*Kübel* at front and rear and can be pulled up over the vehicle at the approach of enemy aircraft.

Noch zeichnet sich die drohende Invasion Siziliens nicht unmittelbar ab und so wird die Freizeit genutzt, um mit dem VW-Kübelwagen die landschaftliche Schönheit der Insel zu erkunden. Vor einem alten Castell präsentiert sich hier diese "Touristengruppe". Am VW-Kübel ist vorne und hinten ein mit Grasbüscheln durchwebtes Tarnnetz befestigt, das bei Annäherung der gegnerischen Luftwaffe über das Fahrzeug gezogen wird.

Another VW-*Kübel* in front of the backdrop of a mountain village, This *Kübel* distinguishes itself from the previous vehicle by the mounting for an additional gas can that is affixed to the left mudguard.

Ein anderer VW-Kübel vor der Kulisse eines Bergdorfes. Dieser VW-Kübel unterscheidet sich von dem vorherigen durch eine auf dem linken Kotflügel angebrachte Halterung für einen zusätzlichen Benzinkanister.

Here is the same VW-*Kübel* with the camouflage net clearly visible from the front. A cloth cover is mounted over the headlights, leaving only a narrow opening* for the light. The name "Otto" is painted below the headlight – giving names to vehicles was a common practice in many armies. [**Often reffered to as a "Cat's eye" – Transl.*]

Hier ist der gleiche VW-Kübel mit dem Tarnnetz noch einmal gut von vorne zu sehen. Über dem Scheinwerfer ist ein Stoffüberzug gezogen, der das Licht nur durch eine schmale Öffnung austreten lässt. Unterhalb des Scheinwerfers wurde der Name "Otto" aufgemalt, eine nicht unübliche Praxis bei vielen Armeen, seinen Fahrzeugen einen Namen zu geben.

A vehicle destroyed on the winding road by Allied aircraft. A unit's PKW* drives carefully past the still smoking vehicle wreckage. The white point above the recognition mark identifies this as a vehicle of the *Luftwaffe* Division "*Hermann Göring*". [**Personen Kraftwagen – the unit's small staff car – Transl.*]

Auf einer Serpentinenstrasse wurde ein Fahrzeug von der allierten Luftwaffe zerstört. Ein Einheits-PKW fährt vorsichtig an den noch rauchenden Fahrzeugtrümmern vorbei. An dem weissen Punkt oberhalb des Kennzeichens ist es als Fahrzeug der Luftwaffen-Division "Hermann Göring" zu erkennen.

In front of a village that has suffered badly during the air attacks, the wrecks of two military trucks lie off the side of the road.

Vor einem durch die Luftangriffe schwer in Mitleidenschaft gezogenen Dorf, liegen neben der Strasse die Wracks von 2 Militär-LKW.

In the middle of vineyards, a *General* inspects the terrain with a Lieutenant Colonel and a clerk. A Lieutenant has also joined in with them. After the formal military salute follows a personal handshake. Standing atop a stonewall, they confer on the defensive measures to be taken. The *General* is wearing a model 1943 tropical tunic with gilt buttons and the accouterments of a brigadier general, leather belt, breeches and black leather high shaft boots and a tropical field cap with gold cord piping. Of his awards, only the Knight's Cross is visible. The LTC (Lieutenant Colonel) has taken off his tunic and has attached the shoulder boards to his shirt.* The clerk is feeling quite warm, since he has rolled up the sleeves of his shirt and the legs of his tropical shorts. He has rolled down his socks to the upper rim of his tropical shoes, as well. (*"*Slip-on" style shoulderboards – Transl.*]

Inmitten von Weinbergen inspiziert ein General mit einem Oberstleutnant und einem Schreiber das Gelände. Ein Leutnant ist zu ihnen gestossen. Nach dem formellen militärischen Gruss folgt der persönliche Händedruck. Auf einer Mauer stehend beratschlagen sie über die zu treffenden Verteidigungsmassnahmen. Der General trägt die Tropen-Feldbluse Modell 1943 mit goldenen Knöpfen und den Effekten eines Generalmajors, Lederkoppel, Breecheshose, schwarze Leder-Schaftstiefel und eine Tropen-Feldmütze mit goldenen Vorstössen. Von seinen Auszeichnungen ist nur das Ritterkreuz zu sehen. Der Oberstleutnant hat seine Jacke ausgezogen und seine Schulterklappen am Hemd befestigt. Dem Schreiber ist wohl schon recht warm geworden, denn er hat die Ärmel des Hemdes und die Hosenbeine seiner Tropenshorts hochgekrempelt. Auch seine Socken hat er auf die Oberkante der Tropenschuhe heruntergerollt.

A German motorcycle messenger on an Italian motorcycle (recognizable by the Italian fascist emblem marked on the steering fork). The motorcyclist is wearing a pair of shorts together with a *Waffen-SS* camouflage tunic and helmet camouflage cover. The camouflage pattern is the very rarely encountered "palm tree" design. The soldiers of the *Luftwaffe*'s *Hermann Göring* Division received camouflage uniforms from *Waffen-SS* uniform stocks for the fighting in North Africa and Sicily. The motorcyclist is wearing a 98k carbine slung across his back. He has an antique signal horn with a rubber (gas bag) clamped beneath the carbine sling.

Ein deutscher Kradmelder auf einem italienischen Motorrad (erkennbar an dem an der Lenkgabel angebrachten Emblem der italienischen Faschisten). Der Kradmelder trägt zur kurzen Hose eine Tarnbluse und einen Stahlhelm mit Tarnüberzug der Waffen-SS. Der Tarndruck ist das nur recht selten zu sehende sogenannte "Palmen-Muster". Für den Kampf in Nord-Afrika und Sizilien erhielten die Soldaten der Luftwaffen Division "Hermann Göring" Tarnuniformen aus den Beständen der Waffen-SS. Über den Rücken trägt der Kradmelder einen Karabiner 98 k. Unter dem Trageriemen des Karabiners hat er ein antikes Signalhorn mit Gummiblasebalg eingeklemmt.

Opposite: A machine-gunner has taken position with his *s*MG34 (*Heavy* machine-gun MG34*). This is an MG34 model machine-gun mounted on a three-legged tripod with an additional optical sighting mechanism. Without the tripod, the gun was referred to as an "*l*MG" (light Machine-gun). [**An MG34 on a tripod mount was considered to be used in a "heavy" machine-gun role. In this configuration it was given the designation "schweres" (heavy). In German, a mounting system used with a gun or cannon was referred to by the French derived term, "Lafette". Thus the sMG was an MG34 or MG42 machinegun mounted on a tripod Lafette. The non-mounted MG was referred to as a "Light" ("leichtes") Machinegun. A self-propelled gun carriage/mount was known as a "Selbstfahrlafette" – Transl.*]

Gegenüber: Ein MG-Schütze ist mit seinem sMG 34 (schweres MG) in Stellung gegangen. Das ist ein MG 34 welches auf einer 3-Bein-Lafette mit zusätzlicher Visieroptik montiert ist. Ohne Lafette wurde es lMG (leichtes Maschinen-Gewehr) genannt.

Two Grenadiers in the midst of setting up an 80mm mortar. They are wearing the Model 1940 steel helmet in the standard grayish paint used by the Army.

2 Grenadiere beim Einrichten eines 80 mm Granatwerfers. Sie tragen Stahlhelme des Modells 1940 in der grauen Standardlackierung des Heeres.

Opposite: A German flamethrower *Panzer* III, Model *M* in battle. Instead of a cannon, this tank was equipped with a flamethrower. It had a store of 1000 liters [*approx. 164 U.S. gallons – Transl.*] of flamethrower fuel, which could be "shot" out to a range of sixty meters. Smoke grenade launchers are visible on the rotatable turret.

Gegen: Ein deutscher Flamm-Panzer-Kampfwagen III Ausführung M im Gefecht. Anstelle einer Kanone war dieser Panzer mit einem Flammrohr ausgerüstet. Er verfügte über einem Vorrat von 1000 Liter Flammöl, welches bis 60 Meter weit "geschossen" werden konnte. Am Drehturm sieht man auch die Nebelkerzen-Halterungen.

Feldw. de Vrient

The graves of German soldiers killed in action in Southern Italy in October of 1943. After the conquest of Sicily by the Allies, the war in Italy continued on with undiminished ferocity for another year and nine months, until May 1945.

Gräber von in Süd-Italien im Oktober 1943 gefallenen deutschen Soldaten. Nach der Eroberung Siziliens durch die Alliierten ging der Krieg in Italien noch 1 Jahr und 9 Monate bis zum Mai 1945 mit unverminderter Härte weiter.

Right: In this cemetery established by the Germans, fallen opponents were also laid to rest beside German dead. These are the British soldiers Alexander Neil and C. Dobs, who found a soldierly death on July 13, 1943.

Rechts: Auf diesem von Deutschen angelegten Sodatenfriedhof wurden neben den eigenen Toten auch gefallene Gegner beigesetzt. Es sind die britischen Soldaten Alexander Neil und C. Dobs, die am 13.7.1943 den Soldatentod fanden.

Opposite: Sergeant Horst de Vrient was buried where he fell on August 7, 1943, at the age of thirty-five – in the vineyard at the foot of Mt. Aetna. After the war, he was transferred to the German military cemetery Motta St. Anastasia at Catania, where the other German war dead from the battle for Sicily also found a worthy resting place.

Gegenüber: Der Feldwebel Horst de Vrient wurde dort begraben wo er am 7. August 1943 im Alter von 35 Jahren fiel – in den Weinbergen am Fusse des Ätna. Nach dem Krieg erfolgte die Umbettung auf den deutschen Soldatenfriedhof Motta St. Anastasia bei Catania, wo auch die anderen deutschen Kriegstoten der Kämpfe auf Sizilien eine würdige Ruhestätte fanden.

Glossary

This glossary is provided for those who would like some additional background information on German uniforms, equipment, awards and other items. Space limitations dictate that it must be confined primarily to items that appear in the photographs in this book, and it is by no means intended to be all inclusive/comprehensive. Please note that any errors in this section are strictly my own.

ARTILLERY

- Infantry Guns [*Infanterie=Geschütze*]
- 76.2mm FK 295/ l (r) [*7,62cm Feld=Kanone 295/l (r)*]
- 87.6mm Field Gun 280 (e) [*8,76cm Feld=Kanone 280 (e)*]
- 105mm Field Howitzer 18 [*10,5cm Feld=Haubitzer 18*]
- 120mm

The Germans used a variety of guns in Africa, some of which were used primarily by infantry troops in direct support (in this case known as an "Infantry gun" – *Infanterie-Geschütz* – of which there were both *light* and *heavy* types), while others were used by soldiers in the Field Artillery branch, including the 88mm gun (most 88s in Africa, however, were under control of the *Luftwaffe* units assigned to the *Afrikakorps* and were employed primarily (at least initially) as anti-aircraft weapons; later they were often employed in a direct fire role against enemy armored vehicles) as well, and earned quite a name for themselves. Other Artillery branch weapons were the Russian built 76.2mm FK 295 /l [r] (this was a captured weapon employed by the Germans), the 105mm Field Howitzer 18, and the largest caliber weapon employed in Africa, the 210mm. As well as the guns captured from the Soviets, captured British weapons were also pressed into use, one being the 87.6mm FK 280 (e) (the letter in parenthesis indicated the country of origin for captured equipment – "r" for Russland – Russia, and "e" for England). The smaller sized German artillery pieces were generally horse drawn, while the larger pieces were pulled by "prime-movers" – that is, a vehicle with the capacity to haul the large, wheeled gun carriages bearing these heavy weapons; one such vehicle was the SdKfz 9 "Famo" – an open-topped halftrack with two front wheels, and a tracked rear section, which could carry most of the gun crew in seats at the back, as well as tow the equipment.

An excellent German website for additional information and technical data on these weapons is available at: http://www.lexikon-der-wehrmacht.de/inhaltsverzeichnis1.htm

AWARDS

The German military was very cognizant of the fact that awards were conducive to maintaining high morale. German military tradition had long followed a practice of awarding various devices designed to recognize a soldier's skills, experience, and courage. These decorations were visually impressive, and thus were most effective if displayed on the uniform, even on combat uniforms in the field. In this way, an individual's courage, combat experience, and level of ability in certain military skills could be identified at a glance. Most German military medals were awarded for combat bravery. The trend for some of the higher awards such as the German Cross, was for approval justified more by a series of actions, rather than for a single specific incident. In other words, you had to prove that your bravery was a repetitive mindset, rather than the result of a decision taken during a single chance event. With fighter pilots in the *Luftwaffe*, the highest awards were presented rather on an "achievement" basis – keyed to a specific kill count. As a result, the number of kills required to win a specific high-level award drifted upward constantly as German pilots pushed their kill levels to new heights.

MEDALS: The Germans felt that the most visually impressive award position was a display at the neck, and so the highest awards were worn suspended from the neck by a ribbon. Medals of this caliber were considered to be the "Knights Cross" level of a given award – for example, the *Ritterkreuz des Eisernen Kreuzes* (Knight's Cross of the Iron Cross). Perhaps the most well known of all German awards – this was the crowning level, so to speak, of the Iron Cross award series. The "Knight's Cross of the War Merit Cross" [*Ritterkreuz des Kriegsverdienstkreuzes*] was similarly, the crowning level of the War Merit Cross series, which also included a lower level 1st and 2nd Class award (as well as the distinction of being "with" or "without" swords).

The Knights Cross level of an award was generally a.) *slightly larger than the lower level awards in the series,* and/or b.) *made using genuine silver* (i.e. higher quality materials).

Lower level, more standard medals for courageous actions were usually worn centered on the breast pockets (this was the position of most importance at the lower level). Such awards did not have an associated ribbon (the medal was always worn).

German military tradition had long favored the left breast pocket, and thus the Iron Cross First Class was always worn here. The War Merit Cross 1st Class (with, or without swords) could also be worn here, though the EK I. took precedence. The German Cross, introduced in 1942, as a higher award, was assigned to the right breast pocket.

The lowest level medal for courageous action was usually awarded as a medal with an accompanying ribbon. Once the award was made, however, only the ribbon was actually worn in the field (almost always attached through the second buttonhole of the tunic, and extending to the edge of the tunic closure). The ribbon for the World War I Iron Cross 2nd Class was also worn here. There were a few other campaign medals that were worn this way (without the medal) – for example, the Eastern Front Medal, and the "West Wall" medal, while the actual medal itself, on a stiff-backed (mounted) ribbon, would only be worn again on a parade uniform.

BADGES/CLASPS: The Germans also issued badges/clasps that represented a soldier's combat experience – his proficiency in combat – within a particular type of fighting such as "Close Combat" (i.e. with no heavy weapon support, and no fortifications), Panzer (tank) battles, infantry battles, general offensive combat under specific qualifying conditions (General Assault Badge – *Sturmabzeichen*), and the like. Among this type of badge was also included the Wound Badge series (similar to the U.S. Purple Heart).

These badges or clasps were also often of complex and detailed design, and in some cases involved a system with three achievement levels (represented by Bronze, Silver and Gold colored finishes). Such awards were affixed to the tunic by means of a built-in pin of some sort on the back, which was inserted through thread "loops" sewn onto the uniform for just this purpose (after the award was received). These badges were usually worn on the left breast, below and to each side of, any medals for bravery already held by the soldier (except for the prestigious "Close Combat Clasp" series, which was worn horizontally above the left breast pocket). The Army's badges for combat experience (e.g. Panzer Assault Badge, Infantry Assault Badge, etc.) were awarded only after the individual completed a specific number of engagements under specific conditions. *Luftwaffe* combat badges included the *Luftwaffe* Ground Assault Badge and the *Luftwaffe FlaK* (anti-aircraft) Badge. For these badges, the individual's qualifying experience was tallied up in his personal records files, until the requirements for the award were met.

Operational "Qualification" Badges: The *Luftwaffe* also awarded a number of badges that indicated the wearer was certified as a qualified (licensed) pilot (i.e. the Pilot's Badge), or pilot and observer (Combined Pilot/Observer Badge), or as a paratrooper who had completed the requisite number of training jumps (Paratrooper Badge), for example. These badges were associated with operational or practice actions, and did not require any engagement with the Enemy – yet they were still very well made, and no less attractive than the badges awarded for actual combat.

AWARDS for Bravery/Combat Prowess, in Order of Significance *[incl. Location of wear]*

Oak Leaves, Swords, and Diamonds to the Knights Cross of the Iron Cross (*Eichenlaub mit Schwertern und Brillanten zum Ritterkreuz des Eisernen Kreuzes*)
[Worn at the neck above the Knight's Cross] – This was essentially the highest German award (there was actually one higher – this having with the Oak leaves struck from gold, rather than the normal 835 or 900 silver – but this special award was awarded only one time, and was specially made for this particular case; the recipient was a *Stuka* pilot named Hans Ulrich Rudel). Presented by Hitler.

Oak Leaves and Swords to the Knights Cross of the Iron Cross (*Eichenlaub mit Schwertern zum Ritterkreuz des Eisernen Kreuzes*)
[Worn at the neck above the Knight's Cross] – 2nd highest award. The highly detailed, crossed swords were attached to the bottom of the Oak leaves. Presented by Hitler.

Oak Leaves to the Knights Cross of the Iron Cross (*Eichenlaub zum Ritterkreuz des Eisernen Kreuzes*)
[Worn at the neck above the Knight's Cross] – 3rd highest award. The oak leaves were made of 835 or 900 grade silver in most cases, though rare examples appear with the oak leaves struck from Platinum – most likely a special request order. This award came with a large presentation document (hand calligraphy) and a handsome presentation folder. Presented by Hitler.

Knights Cross of the Iron Cross (*Ritterkreuz des Eisernen Kreuzes*)
[Worn at the neck] – 4th highest award, but a far step above the Iron Cross 1st Class. The Knight's Cross could be – and was – awarded for single acts of exceptional bravery, or for a series of actions that exhibited both exceptional courage and combat skill. The trend was for the former, though the latter also occurred. Among *Luftwaffe* pilots, award of the Knight's Cross was more often associated with an individual's combat prowess as evidenced by his achieving a set number of enemy aircraft "kills". The number of kills required to win the award, however, increased dramatically during the course of the war as the impressive scores of several extremely successful pilots constantly drove the required number to ever-higher levels. Hitler personally presented the award whenever possible, but as the war progressed, this became increasingly difficult to accomplish.

The Knight's Cross was presented with a large, handsome award document (certificate), housed in a hand-tooled red-leather presentation folder. The document was made of thin, stiffened sheepskin vellum, with the presentation details rendered in superb calligraphy (all the awards were prepared by the same calligrapher, a woman named Frieda Thiersch). All awards at the Knight's Cross level and higher were presented in a presentation folder of some sort, called a "Mappe". While the Knight's Cross *Mappe* was red leather with gold insignia and highlights, the Mappe for higher awards was in white leather; these folders were even fancier – and all were made with the same superlative craftsmanship.

Two excellent references are available for more information on these awards; see: *The Iron Cross of 1939* by Gordon R. Williamson, or *The Iron Time* by Stephen Thomas Previtera.

German Cross in Gold (*Deutsches Kreuz in Gold*)
[Worn centered on the right breast pocket] (Note: There was also a version of this award in *Silver*; both versions were also available in cloth, on a number of different backing colors).

According to the view of Mark Yerger, author of: *The German Cross in Gold, Holders of the Waffen-SS and Polizei*, the German Cross was an independent award – not an award that was merely part of the Iron Cross series (i.e., mid-way between the higher level Knight's Cross and the lower level Iron Cross 1st Class, as some people suggest). There was, in fact, no requirement that one must hold the German Cross prior to winning the Knights Cross. In fact, some Knight's Cross winners never won the German Cross. It *was* a requirement, however, that for an individual to be recommended for the German Cross in Gold, he *must already have been awarded the Iron Cross 1st and 2nd Class*, as a pre-requisite for qualification. Unlike the Knight's Cross, which was often awarded for a single extraordinary act of courage, the recommendation trend for the German Cross award was for a *series of exemplary actions* that repeatedly demonstrated the recipient's propensity to achieve well over the mark. The German Cross was an impressive decoration, with a very complex, multi-piece design. The final award was a handsomely crafted piece, but also quite heavy. Some soldiers/officers did not like the weight – or else felt that the fairly large size of the badge and its many pointed projections made it easy for the award to get hung up on a tank turret hatch, or on equipment or lines within an aircraft, for example – especially when worn on a shirt pocket. For this reason, a cloth version of the award was also produced, which was very lightweight, yet still quite impressive. It was sewn to the center of the right tunic or shirt pocket, and snagging problems were almost completely eliminated. The cloth award was produced on a field gray wool backing for Army and Waffen-SS personnel (continental uniform), and on a black backing for wear on the black wool Panzer uniform; it was also produced with a bluish gray backing for wear by *Luftwaffe* personnel whose continental uniforms were in this color. The German Cross award was referred to by many soldiers as the "Fried Egg" award, and some individuals did not entirely appreciate the large swastika image.

Iron Cross 1st Class
Worn only as a medal (there was no ribbon with this award) *Eisernes Kreuz I. Klasse* [centered on the left breast pocket] of all uniforms (on Navy *"EK I")* uniforms there was no pocket, but the position remained the same).

1939 Spange
An individual who had received the Iron Cross 1st Class in World War I would not receive another cross if he won one during World War II; instead, he received a "Spange" (*Clasp*) to wear on the pocket just above the World War I cross. This Spange was a silver eagle perched on a box with the date "1939". The Spange usually had a flat reverse, with a pin and catch. The pin passed through thread loops on the front of the pocket.

Iron Cross 2nd Class
This was the lowest award form bravery and was awarded *Eisernes Kreuz II.Klasse* together as a medal with ribbon during the ceremony; on the *("EK II")* field uniform, however, it was displayed only as a ribbon, attached to the bottom edge of the second buttonhole. (*The actual Medal was usually sent home, and was only worn on a dress tunic*).

1939 Spange II. Klasse
A person awarded the EK II during the "Great War" (World War I) wore the World War I Imperial ribbon in his second buttonhole. This ribbon was colored black and white, unlike the World War II EK II. ribbon (*which was black, red and white – i.e. the colors of the national flag*). If awarded the EK II again in the Second World War, he received a 2nd Class Spange, which was worn affixed to the ribbon, by four prongs on the back. The design was otherwise the same as the EK I. Spange – though slightly smaller. The ribbon was also available in ribbon bar form, for wear on a bar above the pocket.

Campaign Decorations

"Ostmedaille"
(Eastern Officially titled "die Medaille Winterschlacht im Osten 1941 – Front Medal) 1942" (Medal for Winter Combat in the East), but jokingly referred to by the troops as "Gefrierfleisch Orden" (the "Frozen Meat Order"), this was a round medal awarded with a ribbon to those troops who had served in Russia during the specified time period. Worn only as a ribbon (red, with narrow white center stripe and a black pinstripe down the center) on the field uniform, attached to the second buttonhole. The actual medal was worn only on the dress uniform, or as a ribbon on a ribbon bar.

Campaign Shields
Campaign shields were exactly that – shield-shaped metal awards on a wool backing that bore a motif associated with a given campaign; this included the name of the campaign and the valid campaign dates (beginning and end). These shields were worn on the left upper sleeve of the uniform. They were mounted on a wool-felt backing cloth, in the color of the Branch of service (e.g. field gray for Army and Waffen-SS, bluish gray for the *Luftwaffe* uniform), and also in a black backing for wear with the black Panzer uniform. These shields could be worn even when the individual was no longer serving in the theater where it was earned. Most of these shields were awarded for battles that occurred in Russia, though the very first was awarded for the campaign in Norway. Thus, someone assigned to the African theater, or Sicily, from a prior assignment that included one of these campaigns, may have been entitled to wear such a shield. Among the most significant official shields were:

Narvik [Narvikschild] 1940
The Narvik shield was the first campaign shield to be created. Instituted in August of 1940, it was issued to all *Wehrmacht* troops (regardless of branch of service) who took part in the landings and battles leading to the capture of Narvik, Norway.

Cholm [Cholmschild] 1942
This shield was instituted in July of 1942 in commemoration of the heroic defense of Cholm against a numerically superior enemy force, and was awarded to all *Wehrmacht* military and attached personnel who took part in the defense of Cholm between 21 January and 5 May of 1942.

Krim [Krimschild] 1942
The "Krim" Shield (Crimea Shield), instituted on July 25, 1942, was awarded to all military soldiers and attached personnel who took part in the battle for the Crimea in the Ukraine between September of 1941 and July of 1942, and met the award requirements. (This shield was awarded through General von Manstein).

Demjansk [Demjanskschild] 1943
Created on 25 April 1943, and awarded to all *Wehrmacht* military personnel who took part in the defensive battles in the area around Demjansk during 1942. This shield would not have appeared in Africa, due to the time frame.

Kuban [Kubanschild] 1943
Instituted in 1943, this shield was another shield for actions in Russia, and was awarded to all *Wehrmacht* troops who fought in the battles for the Kuban bridgehead in 1942. Another shield that is unlikely to have ever appeared in Africa, since it was created in 1943.

There was no shield ever awarded for the campaign in Africa.

Combat Badges

Panzer Assault Badge: The accepted English translation of this award title is actually [Das Panzerkampfabzeichen] incorrect. "Kampfabzeichen" means "combat badge".

For tank crews and men of the Panzer branch, this badge was silver. It was worn on the lower part of the left breast pocket – or that area if there was not pocket. Eligible was any officer, NCO or enlisted man who served in the position of Tank Commander, Driver, Gunner, or Radioman, and who had taken part in a minimum of three tank engagements in one or more of these capacities on three different days (one engagement might have lasted two days, but counted only as one engagement). Armored Infantry troops (*Panzer Grenadiere*), assigned to a Panzer unit (regiment, Division, etc.) could qualify for the award, but received a bronze colored version, not silver.

Infantry Assault Badge: The Infantry Assault Badge was issued to "leg" infantry troops [*Das Infanterie-Sturmabzeichen*] (i.e. men in rifle companies that were not part of a motorized Infanterie-Division – i.e. they could not be *Panzer-Grenadiere*), and who had taken part in 1) three combat assault operations 2) at the front lines, armed with 3) hand held weapons during the assault (small arms) and which took place on three different days. Non-motorized troops were awarded this badge in silver, and it was worn on the lower part of the left breast pocket Any officer, NCO or enlisted man in an infantry unit, who met the specifications listed. Motorized Infantry troops could qualify for this badge, but they received the Bronze version, instead.

General Assault Badge: The "General" Assault Badge appears in several pictures in this [*Das Sturmabzeichen*] book. Like the Panzer Assault Badge, the English title is incorrect, as it reads simply "Assault Badge". It was intended as recognition for soldiers not in the infantry, such as the Assault Artillery troops, for example (i.e. crews of the self-propelled assault gun known as the Sturmgeschütz), and other types of infantry and armored units who did not qualify for the Infantry Assault Badge or the Panzer Assault Badge. The award criteria for the General Assault Badge were the same as those for the Infantry version. The badge was worn on the lower part of the left breast pocket.

Wound Badges: The wound badge series consisted of three classes, with the [*Das Verwundetenabzeichen* lowest being in Black, the mid-grade in Silver, and the highest grade being in Gold. The Black version was awarded for one or two wounds, the Silver for three or four wounds (or the loss of a limb, an eye, etc.), and the Gold for five or more wounds (or loss of two limbs, eyesight, hearing, Death). All three awards were the exact same design, only the color differed. The badge was worn on the left breast pocket, near the lower corner.

BATON

Field Marshal's Baton: German Field Marshals received an individually handcrafted baton as a symbol of their rank. These were very ornate, and of magnificent quality – and for this reason were inappropriate for use out in the field, under field conditions. As a result, a far less fancy for of baton was used by most Field Marshal when in the field inspecting units, and in field command posts planning combat operations. This was usually a black painted, wooden stick (staff). The bottom end was pointed, while the top bore a metal cap with a long, polished metal head that expanded a bit at the top end.

EQUIPMENT: The Germans found that leather was not an entirely satisfactory material for use in the desert, as it tended to dry out and crack quickly. As a result, the leather equipment belt was replaced with an olive green belt made of a tightly webbed cloth (usually called "webbed canvas"). The "Y"-shaped leather shoulder straps that served together with the belt as the Load Bearing Equipment (LBE) on the continent, were also replaced with a webbed version. Officers had a webbed belt as well, with a round buckle, though many officers continued to wear the standard officer's double clawed leather belt as worn on the continent. The other items of equipment (bread bag, canteen, etc. were the same as the continental versions, though in some cases the original colors were altered to olive green. Ammunition pouches remained the normal leather issue.

INSIGNIA

Tropical Insignia: Tropical insignia used in Africa varied depending on which military service it was for. The Army insignia was mostly machine-woven, on a copper brown backing cloth. The machine-woven emblems are very flat, but have a very crisp detail, with each piece nearly a carbon copy of another. The insignia was woven onto a strip of thin rayon cloth (thin cloth was the best ground for a smooth, super tight weave).

ENLISTED MEN'S INSIGNIA

Eagles & Cockade: The *Afrikakorps* (Army) enlisted men's and NCO breast and cap eagles were manufactured using pale blue thread on a copper brown colored rayon backing cloth. An interesting point worth noting is that on the continental field gray wool uniform, the breast eagle (with swastika and wreath) was always worn with the bottom of the wreath being above the top edge of the right breast pocket. On the *Afrikakorps* tropical uniform, however, the tropical eagle was sewn on in a manner that the lower part of the wreath actually overlapped the top edge of the pocket (something that had long been common practice on continental *Luftwaffe* service tunics). The *Luftwaffe* used off-white thread eagle on tan twill cloth for its tropical insignia, and the process employed was machine-embroidery rather than weaving (the *Luftwaffe* seems to have preferred embroidery over weaving, in most cases). The embroidery process produced eagles with a notably higher surface texture. The national cockade was also embroidered, in black, white and red thread on the same copper colored backing cloth. There was also a machine-woven version of the *Luftwaffe* cockade.

Collar Tabs: Collar tabs were manufactured in a pale bluish gray cloth, with copper brown colored column lines. The tabs were usually sewn directly to the collar. On continental uniforms, Non-commissioned officers wore a tress tape border around the edge of the collar and the shoulder boards, to indicate their NCO status. The tress was also manufactured in a matte aluminum (subdued) form for wear in combat conditions, and later it was even woven from a slightly greenish tinted thread for even less reflection. In Africa, the NCO tress was a light, sandy brown color.

Chevrons: The chevrons for the Army ranks of *Gefreiter* and *Obergefreiter* ("V"-shaped chevrons worn on the left sleeve) were made of copper brown cloth, with the sandy brown-colored NCO tress used to form the "V". These were often in short supply, and soldiers often wore the dark greenish blue wool backed continental chevrons as an alternative.

Shoulder Boards: The enlisted man's shoulder boards used in Afrika were made of the same material as the tunic, piped around the edges in cord of the color designated for the individual's occupational branch (pink for Panzer, red for Artillery, etc.). Tress for NCO's was the aforementioned light, sandy brown color.

Hussar Skulls: Since the Panzer troops were unable to wear their mark of distinction – the black Panzer wrapper uniform – they showed their branch by taking the silver Hussar skull (a jawless Death's Head with crossbones derived from an old cavalry emblem) insignia from the collar tabs of the black uniform, which they then mounted on the lapels of their tropical uniforms – this practice was used by all ranks.

OFFICER RANKS

Eagles & Cockade: Army Officer's were authorized to wear their standard continental style breast and cap eagles on the tropical uniform. These were hand-embroidered in aluminum bullion on a dark bluish green wool-felt backing cloth. Some officers wore instead a flatwire breast eagle – machine-woven eagle in aluminum thread on dark green rayon, and many simply wore the pattern for an enlisted man. General officers wore their usual continental eagle (hand-embroidered in gold bullion wire or gold celleon, on dark green felt), or simply wore also the enlisted man's version. *Luftwaffe* officers likewise often wore the enlisted version of the breast eagle (machine-embroidered in off-white thread on tan cloth) rather than the hand-embroidered, aluminum bullion continental breast eagle.

Collar Tabs: Officer Collar tabs worn on the tropical uniform were the continental style, hand-embroidered in aluminum bullion thread on a dark green felt backing, with column lines on the tabs in the individual's branch color. Some officers again, were satisfied wearing simply the enlisted man's style. Tabs. Generals wore their usual red-backed continental tabs.

Shoulder Boards: Shoulder boards worn by *Afrikakorps* officers were the continental type – (matte aluminum braid), with the officer's *Waffenfarbe* (Branch Color) as piping around the outer edge of the board (except the bottom end). Boards were often of the "slip-on" type, allowing them to be easily changed, or transferred to a shirt with shoulder loops.

UNIFORMS

Continental Uniforms

Tunic and Trousers: The German continental uniform (Model 36) was made of wool (there were summer-weight variations that were made of lighter material, as the war progressed), and had a 4-pocket design with center pleats on the pockets and scalloped pocket flaps. It also had a stand-up collar worn closed at the neck (but rarely so in the field). Collar tabs were worn on the collar, these being machine-woven in most cases. The tabs themselves also went through some simplification as the war continued. The national emblem (eagle with wreath and swastika) appeared above the right breast pocket. The initial versions of this tunic had a dark bluish green collar, and the background of all insignia (breast eagle, base color of enlisted man's shoulder boards and rank chevrons, etc.) was also dark bluish green (this was changed later, as well). This dark-backed insignia style is what is referred to in the text as "continental" insignia, in most cases). The tunic had a 5-button front, the buttons being pebbled aluminum painted field gray. The tunic was simplified several times during the war, with the dark green collar being one of the first things to go (1940) – it was changed on the "M40" tunic to the same color as the uniform material. Pocket pleats and flap scallops were also eventually discontinued. Combat trousers were also made of wool; they were either a completely straight-legged pattern, or had a slight inward taper toward the ankles (these being called "Keilhosen").

Helmet: The German helmet had three distinct model, named by the year in which the models were introduced. These were the Model 35 (M35) helmet, the Model 40 (M40), and the Model 42 (M42). In all three cases, the changes were made primarily as a utilitarian means of simplifying production and only with the M42, where the lower rim ceased to be "rolled" around the bottom and to the inside, of the shell, was there any readily noticeable difference between them to the casual observer. Most of the helmets used in Africa in the first two years were M35s and M40s, with the M42s arriving in 1942.

Special Uniforms

Assault Gun Uniform: The uniform authorized for wear by Assault Gun crews, and later also for the Self-Propelled gun crews in the Armored Infantry (*Panzer-Grenadiere*) was the same cut as that for the Army black Panzer uniform – but made instead of field gray wool. Though these vehicles looked like a turret-less tank, the Assault guns were actually part of the Artillery Branch (i.e. *Sturmartillerie*), not Armor (Panzer), and so the collar tabs on this uniform were the same rectangular tabs with the jawless Hussar skull as used on the Panzer uniform, but the felt face of the tabs were dark green (instead of black) in this case, and the tabs were piped in the bright red *Waffenfarbe* (branch color) of Artillery.

Panzer Uniform: Panzer crewmen were issued a special two-piece uniform (tunic and trousers) made of black wool, as a distinctive sign of their membership in the elite Panzer branch. They also received the standard four-pocket field gray service/field tunic. The Panzer tunic was a wrap-around garment, with the closure buttons secured through a hidden cloth buttonhole tape along the outer edge of the wrapper's left side. The right side was wrapped around first, with the left side laid over it. There were no exterior pockets, and the tunic had a very snug, waist length fit. The collar tabs on this uniform were not the usual columnar type, but were instead rectangular tabs, with a black felt surface and a single silver, jawless "Hussar" skull centered on each tab (this was traditionally a Cavalry emblem). The tabs were piped in the pink cord (Panzer branch color was "*Rosa*" - pink) for Panzer troops, as were the shoulder boards, however, an soldier from, let's say, the Signal Corps, who was serving in an Armor unit, was authorized to wear the Panzer uniform – but with lemon yellow piping on his collar tabs and shoulder boards rather than pink.

The panzer trousers tapered inward at the ankles. They were usually worn bloused, with lace up ankle boots (some soldiers wore the regular leather marching boots). The standard Army field gray garrison cap (*Feldmütze* – field cap) was also provided in a black wool version (and so was the officer M38 garrison cap). The later, cloth-visored M43 field cap (*Einheitsfeldmütze*) was also provided in black. When a visor cap was worn with the black uniform, regulations required that it be field gray – there was NO black visor cap). Note that *Panzerjäger* (Antitank troops) were part of the Panzer branch—despite the fact that their primary mission was to destroy tanks—and so the crews of self-propelled anti-tank guns (like the *Jagdpanther* – 'Hunting Panther'), also wore the black Panzer uniform with pink piping. In Africa, the black wool uniform was impractical, and so the uniform worn was the same as that worn by every other member of the *Afrikakoprs* – except that many tank troops took the Hussar collar tab skulls from the wrapper, and affixed them to the lapels of their tropical tunics, so as to identify themselves more distinctly as Panzer troops.

Tropical Uniforms

Tunic: The German *Afrika* Corps was issued tropical uniforms that were cut in the same manner as the continental uniform, but worn usually with the collar open. The uniform material was cotton twill, since the wool continental uniform was totally unsuitable for tropical, arid conditions. The 4-pocket tropical *DAK* (*Deutsches Afrikakorps*) tunic has 4 pockets, with center pleats and scalloped pocket flaps. The front closure buttons were still pebbled aluminum, but painted olive green. The uniform color was an olive green, but there was a considerable variations in dyes depending on the maker, and after a brief time of exposure, a new uniform item worn with an older, sun-bleached piece showed radical color differences. There was also a significant difference in color between *Luftwaffe* uniforms, and their Army cousins, as the *Luftwaffe* chose a lighter, more sand-colored tan tone for its uniform. Some of the *Luftwaffe FlaK* units assigned to direct supporting duty with *DAK* units were initially issued Army uniforms (one surmises that the Army version insignia was replaced with the *Luftwaffe* type). Shoulder boards on the tropical uniform could be sewn into the shoulder seam, but most common was a set of loops at the shoulder seam that allowed boards with a cloth tongue on the underside, to be slipped through the loop at the base and be secured with a button at the top – hence the term "slip-on" boards.

Shirt: The tropical shirt (the breast eagle was not worn on the shirt) was a pullover type, and was also fitted with cloth loops at the shoulders to allow the wear of slip-on boards when in "shirt sleeve" uniform mode. Collar tabs were not worn on the shirt.

Trousers, Breeches and Shorts: The *DAK* troops were issued with olive green tropical breeches, which were worn with high-shaft, lace up boots; the breeches are considered to be part of the "early"-style of *DAK* uniform. The breeches were fairly tight fitting, and thus did not enjoy much popularity among the enlisted soldiers who had served for a time in Africa. More popular was the tropical version of the straight-legged trousers, since the slight bagginess of the cut offered more comfort, and cooler wear. These trousers were usually worn with the lace up ankle boots and gaiters (*Gemäsche*), though sometimes the continental leather marching boots were used. *DAK* troops were also issued with a pair of shorts which had a so-called "hidden" waist belt – this because only the ends of the belt were visible – which were worn with socks and the lace-up ankle boots. It should be noted, however, that one of the more striking aspects of the German troops in Africa was that "regulation" wear rarely existed – whatever was to hand (and clean) was often mixed and matched with little concern for official regulations.

Luftwaffe troops had trousers that were easily recognizable by their single, large pouch-style thigh pocket, which was closed by a flap with button. These proved quite popular in the field, and even Army troops sometimes wore them if they could get hold of a pair. The *Luftwaffe* also wore shorts, though the cut and pocket positioning differed slightly from the Army pattern.

HEADGEAR

Visor Caps

ARMY: Visor caps worn in *Afrika* by Army personnel were the continental (i.e. [*Schirmmütze*] field gray cover with blue green cap band) type – there was no tropical version of the visor cap in official use (private purchase examples with tan colored tops may have existed). All caps except those of Generals were piped around the crown, and around the top and bottom of the sweatband, in cord colored the individual's *Waffenfarbe* (branch color). All General's caps were piped in gold cord.

Enlisted men's caps, from Private through senior NCO ranks, had a chinstrap in black leather. Officers, from 2nd Lieutenant up through full Colonel, had twisted aluminum chin cords. The insignia for enlisted men, NCO's and Officers up through the rank of colonel, was silver colored, and usually made of metal. General's visor caps through 1942, was also silver, but from 1943 onward, General's insignia was changed to gold. Exceptions existed where Generals wore an officer grade visor cap (not a General's cap).

LUFTWAFFE: *Luftwaffe* personnel also wore their continental visor caps (grayish blue colored cover, black ribbed cap band) in Africa, however some individuals wore a white-topped summer version of this cap. The bluish gray continental cap was piped in the individual's branch color (crown and cap band) for enlisted men and NCO's, while all officer caps from 2nd Lieutenant through full Colonel were piped in aluminum cord. Insignia was silver colored metal for enlisted and NCO ranks, with a leather chinstrap. For officers (Lieutenant through Colonel), the insignia was done in hand-embroidered aluminum bullion thread, and the cap had twisted aluminum chin cords. General's caps were piped in gold cord and had gold colored insignia, with twisted gilt chin cords. The white-topped summer cap was not piped around the white crown, but in all other respects was the same as the regular blue cap.

Field Cap: German Army troops serving with the *Afrikakorps* were issued with a tropical [*Feldmütze*] version of the continental garrison cap known as the M34. The M34 cap was made of wool, while the tropical cap of olive green cotton twill. Here again, there was a considerable degree of color variance. The cut was the same, having side skirts that curved down (scallop) at the front to form a narrower front section. The national colors cockade insignia was applied to this narrow front section, while the national emblem (eagle) was applied to the front of the cap itself, above the scallop. The insignia was the tropical type, with the eagle machine-woven in light blue on a copper brown colored backing, and the national cockade in black/white/red on copper brown rayon. Above the cockade, an inverted "V" chevron, called a "soutache", was applied, in the color of the wearer's branch. New regulations required its removal by 8 September, 1942, but this order was frequently ignored.

The great majority of Army "field caps" were lined in a deep red colored cloth, and had an oilcloth insert between the outer layer of the cap, and the lining, around the bottom as a means of reducing sweat bleed-through. Officer caps were piped around the top crown seam in aluminum mesh cord, and around the curving scallop at the lower front of the cap as well, while the General's cap was similarly piped – but in gold cord. *Luftwaffe* troops also had a tropical version of their own continental garrison cap (*Fliegermütze* – "flyer's cap"), with embroidered insignia as described in the insignia section. The officer's version was piped in aluminum cord around the top edge of the side skirt, but usually used the enlisted men's insignia.

Field Cap M41: ***Army:*** The most commonly seen cap in Africa was the tropical M41 visored. [*Feldmütze* M41] field cap. This much-loved cap style was developed from the Mountain Cap (*Bergmütze*) already used in the German Army – which itself was derived from an originally Austrian design. The M41 had the same standard red color liner as in the garrison cap, and was made from the same type of olive green cotton twill fabric, though the veterans who had spent time in Africa tended to bleach the color to a very pale shade as a sign of their "Old Boy" status. The cap body was cut similar to the garrison cap – that is, with a side skirt shape – but the skirt was only simulated. The visor was quite long, to provide adequate protection from the sun. The "national colors" cockade insignia was applied to the lower front section and above the cockade, a "soutache" in the color of the wearer's branch was also applied (until the regulations of 8 September, 1942 required its removal, though again, this regulation was frequently ignored). The national emblem (eagle) was applied to the upper front of the cap itself, above the scallop line. The insignia was again the tropical type, with the eagle machine-woven in light blue on a copper brown colored backing. Air vent grommets in the cap's upper side enabled some air circulation. Officer caps were piped around the top crown seam in aluminum mesh cord, and some also had piping around the curving scallop at the lower front of the cap as well, while the General's cap was similarly piped – but in gold cord. Quite a few officers (Generals included), for whatever reasons, chose to wear the enlisted man's version of the cap instead (i.e. with no officer piping).

Luftwaffe: At the start of the African campaign, *Luftwaffe* troops in Africa did not have their own version of the M41, and so either went without, or "loaned" one from Army stocks, replacing the Army insignia with the *Luftwaffe* form. Later caps did not differ a wit from the Army pattern, except in the insignia.

VEHICLES

German Vehicles

Following is a brief overview of some of the German vehicles most commonly encountered in the pictures.

Some nomenclature is necessary, in order to better understand some of the vehicle names. German *tracked* vehicles bore the identification "***Sonderkraftfahrzeug***" (Special Motorized Vehicle), abbreviated "SdKfz". This was an inventory designation, and was used alongside the vehicle name, and any model code. Thus, a Tiger I for example, might be "SdKfz 181, *Panzerkampfwagen* VI, Tiger-Panzer I (Ausf. E) – the inventory identification was "Special Motorized Vehicle No. 181, and then the model within its vehicle family "Tank (type) VI" (often referred to as "Mark..." in English) followed by the colloquial name "Tiger-Panzer", and finally, by any "version" code (*Ausführung*), which was identified alphabetically, e.g. Ausf. E, or Ausf. F.

Armored Personnel Carriers

The German's standard APC (Armored Personnel Carrier) was the half-tracked, open-backed SdKfz 251 (this being the vehicle designation). The Germans called this type of vehicle a "*mittlerer Schutzenpanzerspähwagen*" (medium weight armored reconnaissance vehicle). It was easily recognizable with its long nose and flat, front armored radiator and steeply angled side hull armor plates. The SdKfz 251 was produced in a wide range of models for diverse uses, each with its own special model code following the vehicle designation (e.g. Model C – "*Ausführung* C"). The command version of this vehicle family was designated the "SdKfz 263" and was instantly recognizable by the large open framework antenna above the vehicle that ran from front to back. Rommel is often seen in pictures, riding in this type of vehicle. The driver's compartment in the 251/263 vehicles was closed in, with armored front window shields (could be raised upward); the rear bed over the halftrack was open-topped on most models.

Kübelwagen

The German equivalent of the U.S. "Jeep", the "*Kübel*" (Tub) as it was known by the troops, was used throughout the German army, and was designed by Volkswagen based on the Chassis of the original VW Beetle. It was starkly utilitarian, but had a very distinctive shape. The tires were quite narrow, but with larger "balloon tires" issued in 1942, it's terrain capability increased. Unlike the U.S. jeep, the *Kübel* did not have four-wheel drive, and thus was never quite as versatile a vehicle as its Jeep counterpart.

Panzerkampfwagen (PzKfw) – "Armored Fighting Vehicle/Car" (Tank)

The German Panzer arm has long held a famous reputation, mostly due to later tank models that drew much attention because of their nearly impenetrable armor, and formidable firepower. The first exclusively German tank designs, however, were not as effective, and differed considerably from later designs. A characteristic feature of German tank design is that the toothed sprocket wheel, which drives the track, is always at the front on German tanks (on the U.S. M4 Sherman as well, though other U.S. tanks put the sprocket wheel at the rear – now the standard – along with the transmission and final drive). The track system on the early German tanks was in a form known as "*live track*", in which small, fixed "support rollers" – i.e. roller wheels – hold up the track on the upper leg of its route (forward), while slightly larger road wheels with a suspension system, run on the lower section (which lays against the ground). This is the system of choice for most World War II American medium/heavy armored vehicles (but not for the smaller, Chaffee light tank). The liability of a "live" track system is that it tends to present a gap between the bottom line of the support roller wheels, and the tops of the road wheels, where the lower hull side is actually exposed. The Germans employed a system of steel side skirts to protect this area, which, when available, were mounted on the sides of the tank to hang down over the track area and cover this open space (the modern U.S. main battle tank M1 series uses the same system of side skirts).

Subsequent German tank design (e.g. Panther, Tiger), which was greatly affected by the appearance of the speedy and highly maneuverable Soviet T-34 tank with its Christie-style suspension, shifted to a completely different track system known as *"dead track"*. With a "dead track" system, there are no return rollers; the track rests directly against the much larger-sized road wheels on both top and bottom. The overall track length is usually shorter with this system, and the preferred track tension is different.

The Germans produced some very powerful tanks during the war, but instead of concentrating production on one or two of the best designs (and working out the drive train bugs), they continuously split up production into an increasingly larger variety of self-propelled Assault Gun designs and self-propelled Anti-Tank guns (built on the tank chassis), as well as producing ever larger, more heavily armored vehicles at a time when material shortages could least support such experimentation and variety. In addition, German tanks were somewhat over-engineered (particularly the drive system) – they were simply too complicated and it took too long to produce a single vehicle, while the Russian T-34 on the other hand, or the U.S. M4 Sherman may not have been pretty - but could be produced very quickly.

Panzer III (PzKfw III)
This vehicle was the third model of tank fielded in full production by the Germans, which remained in use until around 1943, and in some areas even later. By 1940, however, it was already outdated and outgunned by some opponent vehicles, and hopelessly outclassed by the Soviet T-34/76 in Russia. It remained the most common tank in use by the Germans in the African theater. It was not heavily enough armed, according to many tank men's accounts, but had the advantage of being relatively fast.
Armament: In Africa, these vehicles probably were equipped with the 50mm (short barreled) gun "KwK39 L/ 60", and a bow-mounted MG-34 machine-gun.

Panzer IV (PzKfw IV)
The "Mark IV" vehicle, with a crew of five, was the next stage in development of the "Panzer" series. It was already in limited production by the start of the war, and was very similar in physical shape (body and turret) to the Mark III. Like the Mark III, it also had a "live track" with support rollers at the top, but the hull was slightly longer, and included a fourth support roller and more road wheels. The track width, like the Mark III, remained narrow, which gave it a less than satisfactory ground pressure ratio on certain types of terrain.

The gun mounted on the early production version of the Panzer IV was short barreled, and thus was not very accurate at longer ranges. The original intent had been to use this tank in support of infantry, but with the need to take on enemy armor directly becoming a critical task, the Panzer IV cannon was soon upgraded to the more powerful, higher velocity, long barreled 75mm KwK 40/L43 model gun (with a double baffle muzzle break – the muzzle break serving to reduce the weapon's recoil). The Panzer IV's armor skin was also thinner than the crew may have preferred.

Side skirts with a "stand-off" distance (i.e., the skirts were not mounted directly over the hull, or turret armor – there was a space between them) were often hung from the hull sides over the track area, and mounted around the turret, for increased ballistic protection. Extra track links were also often hung about the tank on any open spaces, for even more protection.

Later production Mark IV "G" models (Ausf. G) and all subsequent "H" and "J" models of this tank were fitted with the slightly longer barreled 75mm KwK 40/L48 gun, which gave increased range and even more accuracy. The "Mark IV" was the "backbone" tank of the German Army through much of the war, but there were never as many available in Africa as there were of the Mark III.

The Panzer IV chassis served as a base for many other vehicles, including several anti-aircraft artillery weapons, such as the *"Wirbelwind"* ['Tornado'] with a Quad 2cm Flak gun system, and the *Möbelwagen* ['Furniture Vehicle'] with a 3.7cm Flak gun; the *"Hummel"* ['Bumblebee'] – a self-propelled artillery weapon. In the Antitank weapon department were the "Jagdpanzer IV" [Hunting Panzer IV] - a self-propelled anti-tank vehicle with a 75 mm PaK (antitank gun), and the *"Nashorn"* ['Rhinoceros'] with an 88mm PaK (antitank gun). The Artillery branch had the Sturmgewehr IV [('Assault Gun IV') also called the "StuG IV"] – which was an assault artillery weapon using a StuG III turret mounting an Assault Gun model cannon – in German, termed a *StuK* – Sturm = Kanone (assault gun) – as compared to a *PaK* – Panzerabwehr = Kanone (anti-tank gun) or *KwK* – Kampfwagen = Kanone (Tank Gun).

Panzer VI (SdKfz 181) Tiger-Panzer ("Tiger-Tank")
Very few Tigers actually served in Africa, and the German Tiger crews had strict orders not to let an intact vehicle fall into enemy hands. This was due to the fact that the vehicle was still something of a secret, having onl;y just been introduced, and it was still an unknown force on the battlefield. The tiger was equipped with an 88mm Tank Cannon (KwK 36 L/56)

Panzerabwehr Kanone "PaK" (Anti-Tank Gun)
The Germans initially used wheeled, towed anti-tank guns with a gun shield (as protection from small arms). These weapons were of calibers up to 75mm (though some Infantry Guns that could also fire anti-tank ammunition, were of larger caliber), with the very early weapons as low as 37mm; these early guns quickly became hopelessly outclassed by better enemy armor, and Antitank guns of less than 75mm generally did not last long on the battlefield since the effective range was too short. During the African campaign, Rommel may have been the first to direct the 88mm antiaircraft cannon to be laid using direct sighting techniques for employment as an antitank weapon – with devastating results. The effectiveness in an antitank role of this superb weapon was quickly noted and its employment in this capacity (with new sights) became a common practice throughout the German military. Eventually, tracked antitank weapons were also developed, consisting of a high velocity, very limited traverse 75mm gun in an enclosed turret section, mounted on a Panzer IV chassis. The first of these tank hunter vehicles – was so named: *"Jagdpanzer"* (Hunting Panzer); its mission was to destroy enemy tanks and armored vehicles. Later models included the *Jagdpanther* – an 88mm anti-tank cannon mounted in a non-moveable turret, built on a Panther (*Panzerkampfwagen* V) chassis, and *Jagdtiger*. Neither of the latter two vehicles saw service in Africa.

Sturmgeschütz
These vehicles were built on the Panzer III and subsequently the Panzer IV chassis, with a non-moveable turret. The *Sturmgeschütz* was, as the name implied, an "Assault Gun" and was intended to provide immediate artillery support to the Infantry. These vehicles were crewed by men of the Artillery branch (not Panzer). The weapon's name was abbreviated *"StuG"* in German, and from this developed its popular, affectionate nickname of *"Stug"* (Stoog). The *Sturmgeschütz* III was armed with a 75mm "Assault Gun" [7,5cm *Sturmkanone* 40/L43, on the Model StuG III F].

Waffenfarbe – Branch Color
There were four branches of Service within the *Wehrmacht* (the German Armed Forces): *Kriegsmarine* (Navy), *Heer* (Army), *Luftwaffe* (Air Force), and the *Waffen*-**SS** (Armed SS). These are organizational branches – Arms of Service – and should not be confused with a soldier's occupational Branch within a given service.

In the Army, for example, there were a large number of occupational branches (*Waffengattung*), each with its own distinct color known as *Waffenfarbe* (branch of arms color). The soldier's occupational branch (Infantry, Armor, Signals, etc., was identified by (1) the piping on his visor cap, (2) Until 1942, by the point up "V" Chevron, known as a Soutache (later discontinued), on the front of the cloth visored tropical field caps; (3) around the edges of his shoulder boards, and (5) initially, by lines of the branch color on his collar tabs (later also discontinued on enlisted men's collar tabs).

The *Luftwaffe* and *Waffen-SS* had branch colors as well, though these did not always correspond with those used in the Army e.g. bright yellow being the Signals Troops branch color used in the Army, but in the *Luftwaffe*, the *Waffenfarbe* for this branch was light reddish brown. There were no operational SS units active in Africa. For this book, the most significant Army and *Luftwaffe* branch colors are:

	ARMY	**LUFTWAFFE**
Armor (Panzer)	Pink	N/A
Artillerie (FlaK)	Bright Red	Bright Red
Fliegender Personal[1]	N/A	Golden Yellow
Fallschirmjäger[1]		
Gebirgsjäger[2]	Grass Green	
Hermann Göring Div*	N/A	White
Panzer-Grenadiere[3]	Light Green	N/A
Nachrichten-Truppen[4]	Bright Yellow	Light reddish brown
Kavallerie (Cavalry)	Golden Yellow	
Nebelwerfer (smoke)	Maroon	
Verwaltung[5]	Dark Green	

1. Flying personnel/Paratrooper 2. Mountain Trooper 3. Armored-Infantry 4. Signals Troops 5. Administration
* This was an elite Luftwaffe ground division, equipped like Army troops.

The branch color was displayed most notably as piping on the shoulder boards, but it also appeared as a soutache on the garrison cap and on the tropical visored field cap (until 1942, when the use of the soutache was discontinued) and as piping on the service dress visor cap (for both Army enlisted men and officers up through the rank of Colonel). It was also used on officer collar tabs, where there are two lines of branch color on each side of a dark green centerline.

WEAPONS

Handgrenades: The German "Stick" (*Stiel*) handgrenade is very readily recognized by anyone even a little familiar with the German Army of World War II. The "*Stielhandgranate* 24" was used by unscrewing the metal cap on the bottom of the stick, pulling on the detonator cord stuffed inside the shaft, and then throwing the grenade. The fuze had only a 4.5 second delay. The Germans also used an "Egg Handgrenade" [*Eihandgranate* 39], which had the friction igniter fuze mounted on the top of the grenade itself. These were the two most commonly used grenade types, with "smoke" versions of the stick grenade available.

Pistols: The usual German side arms included the P-08 "Luger", and the P-38 (***Pistole***) "Walther" (both fired 9mm ammunition). The Germans also used weapons manufactured in factories located in countries that the Germans had occupied, such as the Hi-Power Browning 32 caliber " Pistole 640 (b) '. In addition, captured Allied side arms were also employed.

Rifle: The standard *Wehrmacht* rifle was the 5-shot Carbine (*Karabiner*) 98K, introduced in 1935. The weapon fired a 7.92mm cartridge. Approximately 10 million of these weapons were produced during the Third Reich period (through May of 1945). The weapon had a bolt action, which was used to load the first round into the breech. Captured British and American rifles were also used, when ammunition for them was also available.

Machineguns: The standard German machine-gun in Africa was the MG-34. It was an excellent weapon, but it was also a very highly machined piece, and as is often the case with over-machining, the gun was finicky in anything but the most optimal environment (the high machining also meant that it was time-consuming and costly to produce). This weapon used a 7.92mm cartridge, belt fed (from the left), and the effective rate of fire was 300-400 rounds per minute. The MG-34 had an actual range of approx. 3000 meters – but since the sights were only effective for 2000 meters, the accuracy fell off after 2000. The weapon's barrel could be changed fairly quickly and without too much trouble, from behind the gun – so the weapon could remain in position and the gunner did not have to expose himself to enemy fire in order to disconnect the old barrel and replace it with a new one. The MG-34 was used as the on-board anti-troop weapon in tanks, on armored personnel carriers, and on many other vehicles, including the *Kübelwagen*.

Sub-Machine: In German called a "Machine-pistol" (*Machinenen-Pistole*) and abbreviated Guns**:** "*MP* ", the most well known weapon of this sort on the German's side was the MP-40 ("Schmeisser"). This weapon had a 32 round magazine and fired the same ammunition as used in the Luger and Walther P-38.

Author Bernd Peitz

Bernd Peitz was born in a village near Paderborn where he grew up and still lives today with his wife and three children. After his education in mechanical engineering, he shifted to a position as a design engineer in the furniture production. His interest in the field of military history was awakened quite early by the strong military presence in the area of Paderborn/Sennelager. The many base facilities and the troop training area of Senne, which was used up until 1945 by the German Wehrmacht and since then formed the largest British garrison location in Germany, distinctly [clearly/plainly] mark the environs of Paderborn. As a hobby historian and researcher of his local area, Bernd Peitz has already played an influential role in several exhibitions about the history of the Garrison and about the wartime period of 1939-1945.

The author's particular interest in the German Afrikakorps on the other hand, is based on the fact that his father earlier belonged to this combined arms unit. Whenever possible, Bernd Peitz accompanied his father to the gatherings with his old service comrades, and listened to their experiences from the war. With the support of the Africa Veterans, he also began collecting books, photos, documents, parts of uniforms and bits of equipment from the Afrikakorps. The photos shown in this book were made available to him by the comrades of his father, so that they could be preserved for future generations.

Der Autor Bernd Peitz wurde 1958 in einem Dorf bei Paderborn (/ in Germany) geboren, in dem er aufwuchs und auch heute noch mit seiner Frau und seinen 3 Kindern lebt. Nach seiner Ausbildung im Maschinenbau wechselte er als Konstrukteur in die Möbelherstellung.

Sein Interesse an militärgeschichtlichen Dingen wurde schon früh durch die starke militärische Präsenz im Raum Paderborn / Sennelager geweckt. Die vielen Kasernenanlagen und der Truppenübungsplatz Senne, die bis 1945 von der Deutschen Wehrmacht genutzt wurden und seit dem den grössten britischen Garnisonsstandort in Deutschland bilden, prägen deutlich das Umfeld Paderborns. Als Hobby-Historiker und Heimatforscher hat Bernd Peitz bereits an mehreren Ausstellungen zur Garnisonsgeschichte und über die Kriegszeit 1939 - 1945 massgeblich mitgearbeitet.

Das besondere Interesse des Autors am Deutschen Afrikakorps ist dagegen aus der früheren Zugehörigkeit seines Vaters zu diesem Truppenverband begründet. Wann immer es möglich war, begleitete Bernd Peitz seinen Vater zu den Treffen mit dessen alten Kameraden und hörte sich deren Erlebnisse aus dem Krieg an. Mit Unterstützung der Afrika-Veteranen begann er auch Bücher, Fotos, Dokumente, Uniform- und Ausrüstungsteile vom Afrikakorps zu sammeln. So wurden ihm auch die in diesem Buch gezeigten Fotos von den Kameraden seines Vaters überlassen, um sie der Nachwelt zu erhalten.

Translator and Technical Writer Gary Wilkins

Gary Wilkins comes from the "City of Presidents" Quincy, Massachusetts, and spent his childhood reading historical reference works on the German military, its weapons and soldiers. His long interest in military history led to a major in German language (secondary study in Russian) at the University of Houston, and military service as an Armor officer in the U.S. Army (tanks). Illness forced him to muster out in 1985, as a Captain. Mr. Wilkins moved to Japan, where he lived for seven years. In 1995, he returned to nearby Korea, where he worked at the head office of a Korean petrochemical company in Seoul as an instructor, and as translator and liason for the company in its dealings with German Product Inspection/Testing Certification agencies. He also assisted Japanese business visitors to the company, and worked as a member of the Overseas Sales Team, before returning to the U.S. in 1999. He is the author of *The Collector's Guide to Cloth Third Reich Military Headgear*, and a number of articles written for the *Military Trader* journal. When time permits, he transcribes historical German genealogy documents from the old German script into modern text, with translations. Mr. Wilkins' interest lies in the uniforms, equipment and units of World War II German, American and Soviet tank forces, as well as with the Afrikakorps, its soldiers, and the African Theater. Mr. Wilkins lives with his sometimes resident nineteen-year-old daughter, Jen – who just enlisted in the U.S. Army as a linguist – and with his small, four-legged canine children, Blondie and Geppi.).